FREEDOM FLIGHT

The purpose of this book is to bring the tragic story of nameless and faceless millions of an oppressed era to the mind of the American public that considers freedom a birthright. The story is to serve as a testimony that freedom is not free and when freedom disappears so will the society built upon its premises.

There is no place to escape.

FREEDOM
FLIGHT

A True Account of the Cold War's
Greatest Escape

FRANK ISZAK

New York

FREEDOM FLIGHT

A True Account of the Cold War's Greatest Escape

© 2016 **FRANK ISZAK**.

Published in New York, New York, by Morgan James Publishing. Morgan James and The Entrepreneurial Publisher are trademarks of Morgan James, LLC.
www.MorganJamesPublishing.com

The Morgan James Speakers Group can bring authors to your live event. For more information or to book an event visit The Morgan James Speakers Group at
www.TheMorganJamesSpeakersGroup.com.

Shelfie

A **free** eBook edition is available
with the purchase of this print book.

CLEARLY PRINT YOUR NAME ABOVE IN UPPER CASE

Instructions to claim your free eBook edition:
1. Download the Shelfie app for Android or iOS
2. Write your name in **UPPER CASE** above
3. Use the Shelfie app to submit a photo
4. Download your eBook to any device

ISBN 978-1-63047-826-1 paperback
ISBN 978-1-63047-827-8 eBook
ISBN 978-1-63047-828-5 hardcover
Library of Congress Control Number:
2015916564

Cover Design by:
Alan Munro

Interior Design by:
Bonnie Bushman
The Whole Caboodle Graphic Design

In an effort to support local communities and raise awareness and funds, Morgan James Publishing donates a percentage of all book sales for the life of each book to Habitat for Humanity Peninsula and Greater Williamsburg.

Get involved today, visit
www.MorganJamesBuilds.com

Habitat
for Humanity®
Peninsula and
Greater Williamsburg
Building Partner

How did it happen?

Where was I, what did I do or not do to let it get this far? Who was responsible for this firestorm? Who started it? The more I'd been thinking—and I had a lot of time for that—the clearer the answer became: It was me.

ME!

It would have been easy to say, "I did not see it coming", but I should have. It was my country. It was my decision—or the lack thereof—to let the barbarians rise to power.

The prisons were built; first for the minds and then for the bodies. The insidious disease, Communism, was marching and I was marching along. I believed in false promises and ignored history. Tyranny does not start with the gulags and gas chambers, it ends with them.

I remained silent and hoped that this time it was going to be *different*. I did not yell "FIRE!" when I should have. Now it was too late; the fire was raging, the fire hydrants were dry, and all the firemen were dead.

DEDICATION

You'll be reading my life story with the good, the bad, the trials, the tribulations and enough gratitude owed to fill an entire book. Dedications, however mundane they may sound, are due.

First, to my parents.
They are long gone, hopefully enjoying their afterlives in the eternal kingdom of their beloved Lord, in the dreamland of the justice and fairness they sought, suffered endlessly for, and deserved throughout their lives. May their souls rest in peace.

To my teammates.
Six young Hungarians risking their lives, willingly facing torture and death without hesitation just to have a chance at the ever-elusive, priceless commodity: Freedom.

More specifically two of them: My wife (I call her Anais in the book) to whom I was married for only nine months at the time of our escape. After long deliberations, when I approached her with plans of the escape, there was no hesitation.
All she asked was: "When?"

Then of course, George.
When the chips were down, he performed with superhuman strength
and with an unstoppable determination, unlike any man I ever met.
Had it not been for him, this book would never have been written.
Dead men don't write books.

DEDICATION

A HALF CENTURY LATER

The list of those who made their contribution at various levels of endeavors is longer than space allows me to pay tribute to all. However there are a few who simply must have credit here:

My wife of 21 years, Serpil

Tirelessly churning out thousands of yoga classes to support Silver Age Yoga, our nonprofit "pay back"—the reciprocity for our freedom; thus allowing me time to research and write my book - in fact re-re-write, while make a living by chasing bad guys as a PI and working as Executive Director of the nonprofit.

Unconditional, all around support, that's her specialty.

The literary gurus: Tracy Myers and Jean Kravitz

*Drove them nuts with my style, that **Tracy** called the "Hungarian Shakespeare" version of English—she should know: she is so so English, her bulldogs are named Elliott and Emerson. **Jean's** unwavering support, her blind faith in the potentials of my story was a true confidence booster, characteristically compassionate and forgiving, but when the battles moved* *from typo-hunting and punctuation to the use of words—they both became bloody serious. Each time I prevailed it was time to celebrate. (Chardonnay was our preferred brand. Many a glass later the book got finished.)*

Alan Schueler, the computer genius

For Alan each challenging issue is a "personal war" between him and the computer. He did win each and every encounter with sheer determination, not to mention skill, including the formatting of my book, which was one of his more challenging assignments.

Endre Hules, award winning Hollywood filmmaker

It was pure "serendipity." Filmmakers don't read books offered to them by strangers. Their agents don't either. Endre did, almost by mistake, and fell in love with the cliff-hanger. From there, he never stopped. For over three years he lived the story as much as I did.

Teresa Korniczky, a PR apprentice extraordinaire

A marketing wizard, and a great addition to the team.

TABLE OF CONTENTS

PROLOGUE

THE FRONT PAGES OF NEWSPAPERS AROUND THE GLOBE AND MAJOR MAGAZINES IN THE WESTERN WORLD HAILED OUR ACTION AS A HEROIC ESCAPE FROM TYRANNY TO FREEDOM. The Kremlin-controlled media behind the Iron Curtain referred to the event as "Air Piracy". They would have called it hijacking, but no one had coined the word yet.

In the days following the escape, we sought political asylum in the West. The Justice Department (*Bundesministerium fur Vertriebene, Fluchtlinge und Kriegsgeschadigte*) of the democratically elected Federal Republic of Germany (aka: West Germany) adjudicated our case and granted our request.

In writing this book, I assigned fictitious names to the participants. While most of those mentioned are gone from planet Earth, any reference by their true names, depending on which regime is ruling Hungary at a given time, may adversely affect those, like relatives, still alive. In addition, some of the names have descended into my memory beyond retrieval.

I referred to George by his real name as he was known and quoted by the international news media. My nickname was Zak, even though at the time of the escape I was not using my abbreviated name regularly. The members of the cockpit crew, including the security agent, are mentioned by their true names mostly as part of the translated documents (mostly interrogations) obtained from archives of the Hungarian Historical Society.

Some students of history believe that our escape, which is narrated in *Freedom Flight*, was one of the powerful, albeit indirect, motivators of the Hungarian Uprising; it exploded four months later on October 23, 1956. We demonstrated that tyrants are not invincible. The Iron Curtain, which Winston Churchill most aptly named, and the Communists considered impregnable, had ultimately failed its mission of sealing the twentieth century slave camp known as Hungary, from the West.

THE COLLAPSING PLANS

CHAPTER I

Kelenfold Railroad Station near Budapest
Tuesday, July 10, 1956 1700 Hour

THE HUGE CLOCK APPEARED SLIGHTLY ANGLED TO THE RIGHT ON THE WALL OF THE WAITING LOBBY AT KELENFOLD'S RAILROAD STATION. THE FACE OF THE CLOCK MUST'VE BEEN WHITE, AGES OR RATHER MANY TRAINS AGO. Now it was yellowish-gray. It had black roman numerals; the arms were also black. It showed exactly five o'clock: the train was supposed to have arrived already. Apparently, it was running late.

Not a good sign! I thought.

George and I were the only people waiting for the arrival of the train. The decision to meet Robert at this railroad station, at the southern outskirt of Budapest, was made by George.

"A lot less conspicuous, trust me", he told me when we decided to go together to meet Robert. There was not a lot of argument, George was right. On one hand, I had no idea what Robert looked like and true;

3

Kelenfold was a lot less conspicuous, less attended than the next and final stop of the train: Budapest Eastern Station.

Here we were, waiting for the train bringing Robert and his duffel bag full of "tools". The tools, as we called them, were actually handguns, ostensibly Hungarian Air Force officers' sidearm editions: 9mm Mausers, with plenty of ammunition.

These "tools" were absolutely necessary to carry out our plan, which was supposed to be going down in the annals of aviation as a "first"—the diverting of a commercial airliner on its domestic route, an escape from one of the darkest tyrannies in the history of the twentieth century—from Hungary to the Free World, the West.

Guns were pivotal in carrying out our escape plan.

It was ten minutes past five when the train rolled in on the third track, six passenger cars dragged by a WWII steam engine, huffing and puffing to a stop. Four doors opened. At two of them a couple of conductors appeared; the third door let out an older man holding the hand of a young boy; out of the remaining fourth open door came three middle age women with tote bags in hand.

Where's Robert?

A couple of minutes later the engine was hissing out steam on the front side of the two large horizontal cylinders, the way a black steel dragon would do, if there were dragons. The connecting arms between the axels began to slide forth and back, turning the wheels. The train began to roll out of the station.

I stood there dumbfounded—waiting for a miracle to happen. Maybe the train would stop and track back: *Oops! We forgot to drop off Robert.* The station was now empty; the last image of the train was the tail end of the last car, vanishing into the hazy infinite distance. Vanishing, just like our plan. A well designed plan for sure, just died. The odds of seven of us dying along have just exponentially increased. Bile bitterness flooded over me.

"So there's no Robert, is there?" Anger was pouring out of me. My voice was hollow, seethed with bitterness. The words seemed to come from a faraway place, echoing like pebbles falling on a cobblestone street in the silence of a night.

George did not answer, but it no longer mattered. We were three days away from an event that was destined to become history. As it looked now, it was to become nothing but a sad history of an aborted dream.

CHAPTER II

Arany Bika (The Golden Bull) Beer Bar
Budapest, Hungary
Tuesday, July 10, 1956 2100 Hour

THE NIGHT WAS ALREADY DARK; THE FEW LIGHT BULBS DANGLING FROM TWISTED ELECTRICAL WIRE SPANNING FROM ONE BUILDING TO ANOTHER HARDLY MADE THE NIGHT ANY BRIGHTER. Six of us were sitting around a long wooden table, covered with a polka-dot tablecloth, which must've seen better days. The garden beerhouse was on the Buda side of the metropolis, Budapest, capital of empires for centuries.

Why is this city so dark? I wondered time and again.

Maybe it was the state of mind. Those opulent, distorting lenses— the eyes of the mind, the prisms of the soul—capable of changing the world, adding colors, or taking them off, creating darkness. All depends on their settings. It's the mind that sets those lenses, and mine was not in very good shape. Neither the lenses, nor the mind, that was now slowly drifting in and out of the conversation humming around the table.

We were waiting for George and hopefully, Robert. I already knew the sad news about Robert but I was not about to tell. Those present had no idea that I went along with George to meet Robert, who held our fate in his hand, rather in his probably non-existing duffel bag. Let George tell them. In addition, he may have been able to make a connection with Robert after all, if there has ever been a Robert, and he'll be walking in with him and the seven handguns in his duffel bag.

George came ten minutes later, alone. He sat down without a word between my wife Anais and Charlie.

George was a strange character. He spoke softly in short, sometimes unfinished, sentences but I seldom heard anyone so forceful with words. Just like giving orders without the appearance of giving orders. There was finality to his words, leaving no room for doubts, let alone for arguments. He was medium built, about five ten, powerful shoulders. He kept his head slightly tilted to the right, had a beak-like nose, and a nickname to go with it: Csoros, the "beak-nosed one".

Smalltalk ceased. An ominous silence hovered over the table.

"There are no guns," George said as a matter of fact then added: "and there won't be any!"

Bolla was the largest member in the group, sitting across from me. His head was balding on the front, his short neck descended into wide shoulders. One could mistake him for a professional wrestler, although he was not. He waved at the waiter who slouched against the wall of the building near the kitchen, as if trying to decide whether it was worth making a move, and if so, which direction.

"Bring us a round," Bolla said, then added with visible irritation, "and try to bring it tonight!"

The waiter turned around and maybe out of respect for Bolla's wide shoulders, or maybe because we were the only customers in sight, he returned within a reasonable time with seven mugs of beer. The silence was still with us for quite a while. The beers were just sitting there, untouched, nobody seemed to care. Their white, foamy caps sank and settled, slowly disintegrating into the amber colored liquid below.

"Not a lot left is there?" asked Bolla.

Whether he was referring to the collapsing foam of the beer or to our collapsing hopes, I could not tell. It took some time for the gravity of the news to sink in, but when it did, the sign of devastation actually showed as if was carved on everyone's face. Bolla's words were still reverberating when Charlie spoke.

"Now what?"

The answer came from George:

"Well, we're going back to the original plan!" No apologies, no explanation, no excuse, just new orders.

Back to the original plan. Coming from him it sounded so simple. Like, *Can I have a cup of tea instead of coffee this time?*

The original plan, sure.

George and I dreamed it up about six weeks ago. It sounded simple, at least in the beginning. Actually, we developed two possible versions; an ideal and a realistic one. The ideal one was that George and I were going to secure a couple of guns, board one of the domestic airlines flying west from Budapest as passengers, and at a prearranged time pull our guns, disarm the AVO security agent on board, force the crew out of the cockpit and fly the plane to freedom. This version had only one problem, a huge one: it needed guns. Knowing that getting weapons would be virtually impossible, and if we were caught for possessing one would mean endless years in prison, forced us to devise a second version, a more realistic plan. This one called for a somewhat more complicated arrangement: overwhelming all passengers by sheer force, making sure that the armed AVO agent is amongst them—and disarmed—taking his gun, then the control of the plane. Now this realistic plan needed more conspirators than just the two of us. We knew, or thought we did, the configuration of the seats in the passenger cabin. The number of available passenger seats—according to George—should be seventeen.

Problems quickly arose: how many "bodies" do we need for the take-over, and how to find them?

If the number was too small, we would not have enough people to overwhelm the rest of the passengers. If the number was too large, we faced not one, but two major issues. First, we would become too conspicuous. A dozen young people flying on a commercial carrier, reserved usually for government and Communist Party officials, certainly would not go unnoticed. Second, there was the issue of secrecy. To keep the plan concealed up to the very moment of execution was in adverse relation to the number of people who knew about it. With every new addition to the team, the danger of being discovered grew at an uneven proportion.

After abandoning the first version as not doable, we started recruiting what we believed to be trustworthy conspirators, the "team" now sitting around the table. The realistic plan became the "original plan." It took us a few weeks to recruit the team of seven. The recruits' reaction to the plan was similarly enthusiastic to ours, at least in the beginning. Then, the closer we got to the actual date, although not yet exactly determined, the reality sank in with everyone. The fear of facing an armed AVO (Hungarian version of the Soviet KGB) agent "bare handed" overwhelmed everything else.

The team became jittery, subconsciously suspicious of one another. You could feel desertion looming. Then in late June, maybe it was already July, at one of our late night meetings in Budapest (by the way, for each of our meetings, and there were about six of those, we always met at a different place to avoid suspicion of the ever-present "block-informers") George brought exciting new information; he'd recruited the eighth member of the team, whom he simply called Robert. What was significant about Robert, George explained, was that Robert was not only a highly trusted friend from his Air Force days, but also—*hang on now*—he was a weapon repair and maintenance officer still in the Air Force, having virtually unlimited access to secure any number of handguns, the absence of which weapons would not be noticed for days, if not for weeks!

With the entry of Robert and the seven guns our hopes revived; our spirits lifted and soared. The plan now seemed workable with a reasonable chance to succeed.

Until this evening.

"Let's review this 'original plan' stuff," I said, still harboring the deep disappointment of the letdown at the railroad station. I spoke up first, because I had the most to lose, all our bridges were burned. We were a long way down on the road of no return.

"Here is what I recall of the original plan," I spoke as if to George, but it was for everyone as I now had everybody's attention.

"We encountered at least half a dozen major obstacles - let's see if I can recall them. If I get stuck, George, why don't you help me out?" I said trying to equal his usual sarcasm.

"First we need to identify the AVO agent. Now rather than going into details with the problems with that issue, let me go straight to the next obstacle."

Ignoring my request of no interruption, Anais spoke:

"Is there any clue, any clue at all, who he might be?"

I looked at her. She would be 21 years old by next May, that is, if there was to be a 21st birthday in her future. Right now that did not look very promising. I was extremely frustrated and sounded bitter when I responded.

"Sure there is. They wear signs. Always. It says 'I am a cop'. One on their chest and in case you missed that one, another one on their forehead..." The sarcasm was not called for, I realized as soon as I said it. We were married for nine months. There was no use in hurting each other when there might be only a very short life left.

"Sorry," I said. Then I saw a glint in her eyes, meaning she understood the sincerity of the apology and had already forgiven me.

"What I am saying is," I continued softly, "we have no way to identify the AVO agent, and you know the drill: not knowing which passenger is the armed agent we need to knock out all ten passengers cold, if that's how many there are."

Realizing that I was about to be interrupted again, I decided to let each issue be debated if they wanted to. I started with the challenge:

"Did any of you ever try to knock out two strangers within seconds?" since there was no answer, I continued.

"Let's assume we all turn into action movie stars and wipe out a planeload of passengers in about three seconds, miraculously unearth the AVO agent's gun, load it ready to fire, now what?"

"Break the cockpit door!" said Bolla. Then turning to George:

"What's the door made of?

George, as usual, got around the question instead of answering straight.

"It does not matter. We just knock on the door."

"Oh, yeah," said Bolla "and what do we say, 'good afternoon folks, how is the flight so far'?"

George obviously did not appreciate his authority being questioned. He looked at Bolla with his blink-less eyes long enough to let him know, then told him that the door probably would be opened by a member of the crew, assuming it was the AVO guy wanting to come into the cockpit. Maybe just to chat. They would never even dream that some passengers were going to storm the cockpit with gun in hand.

"After all, it has never happened!" George said with finality.

Now we all had to take George's word for it, for he was a test pilot in the Hungarian Air Force just a few years back, he was supposed to know what's going on "up there". There was no need to ask George how he knew "it", whatever the "it" was. If he wanted to tell, he would have. Questioning him for details or proof would appear doubting his authority needlessly.

So that took care of entering the cabin.

"What if the crew is armed?" I asked George.

"Crossing that bridge" then his voice trailed off, I could not hear the rest of what he said.

*Did he say if we **ever** get there?* I tried to recall, but I could not. Maybe I did not want to. Then of course there were plenty of other issues; wrestling the control of the aircraft in the cockpit, fighting possibly as many as four crew members in tight quarters. Then George flying the plane, unless injured or killed. He would have to avoid radar detection and potential fighter jets from a Russian airbase located only a few miles away from the flight-path. Then fly all the way to West Germany crossing Austria over the Alps without any navigational aids—about two hundred miles. God knows how much fuel the aircraft carries, or what kind of weather would be encountered. The list of seemingly insurmountable and uncontrollable obstacles was endless.

The night was long. The answers were few and vague.

Charlie spoke.

"We better make a decision and make it tonight," he said turning to George, then to me. Charlie's father was a judge in the Communist system that Charlie referred to as a "farce". On the other hand because of his father's position, he had access to all kinds of legal documents including the draconian laws and penalties dealing with the act we were about to commit.

"According to the laws on the books we are committing three crimes," Charlie went on. "One is an attempt to escape Hungary by unlawful means—life imprisonment. The two others are considered treason: applying physical harm to government personnel while attempting to escape—death. Taking illegal possession and/or using any instrument (such as an airplane) considered to be property of the government—death. And to be sure that all fields are covered: using firearms in any escape attempt—death. The death penalty is usually carried out by hanging."

The silence that earlier hovered above the table now invaded everyone's soul. It was frightening.

We suddenly realized what was in store for us if we failed. Charlie, trying to lighten the immense weight of the moment, added:

"By the way, the tortures are not listed. The list would be too gruesome and too long."

Nobody laughed.

George, in his low, somewhat crackling voice threw in the question: "Anyone planning to desert?"

I was 25 years old and had been exposed to enough threats to cover several lifetimes. But I never, ever heard words with so much ominous threat packed into them as these four had. Gabor, a friend from my school days, whom I recruited into the team, spoke, capping the long silence turning toward me:

"What do we have on the other side of the equation, opposite the gallows?"

The answer was in my heart at all times. It invaded every inch of my body it became my entire life.

I did not even have to say it: the word rolled off my lips slowly at an even tone, without emphasis, sounding self-evident.

"Freedom."

There was no need for explanation. Somehow everything became plain and simple. The equation was balanced. It sounded like a huge orchestra was playing it. We knew the price and we were willing to pay it. Someone had to name the price in exchange for our lives.

"Freedom."

***

Around two o'clock in the morning we all left the Golden Bull. The plan to seize the control of the aircraft without weapons, disarming the undercover AVO agent, or agents on board was reviewed, discussed and agreed upon by everyone.

Throughout the evening while we were revising plans, I had already decided that the takeover plan was not good enough, not for me, not without at least one real weapon. For me, the only real weapon was a gun. It was a must, whether for show or for real, and I believed I knew where to get one. I needed a bit of luck and some serious and somewhat dangerous travel.

I walked Anais to a small hotel where we were staying for the last few days, near the Margit Bridge, on the Buda side. At the doorway of our room I kissed her and walked down three flights. It was late night, or early dawn being mid-summer, streetcars were not running yet. I walked all the way to the Southern Railroad Yard in Buda, on the west side of Budapest. The walk took three hours. At the station I bought a round trip train ticket to Vep with most of the money I had.

CHAPTER III

Southern Railroad Yard
Budapest, Hungary
Wednesday, July 11, 1956 0500 Hour

THE TRAIN RIDE TO VEP WHEN ON SCHEDULE, TOOK ABOUT EIGHT HOURS. Vep was a small village about five miles east of Szombathely, which was considered by Hungarian standards a medium sized city. Sprawling at the eastern foothills of the Alps, Szombathely was less than twenty miles inside the Hungarian-Austrian border. The two countries were separated by the Iron Curtain.

It was early.

The train was not scheduled to leave for another hour. I went to the canteen that had just opened, bought a hot sausage and a cup of coffee then went back to the train. The cabin was empty as I sat down by the window.

I kept reviewing the plan again and again. The ultimate object was still the same with or without weapons: disarm the plainclothes AVO agent, and take the control of the aircraft. And try not to hurt, or God forbid, kill innocent passengers or crewmembers in the process. In my mind, the plan with weapons, combined with the element of surprise, had a reasonable chance. Without weapons: more like a foolish suicide.

The train departed on time; it rolled through endless switches out of Southern Railroad Yard. Farther east, above Budaors, beyond the haze of factory smokestacks, the sun was rising.

It was Wednesday, July eleventh, six in the morning.

***

I had eight long hours to contemplate the mind-boggling escape plan. I was so deep in my thoughts I hardly noticed the passing of stations. About three stations short of Szombathely, the usual armed border patrol version of the AVO (called AVH: Border Patrol for State Security) came through checking every passenger for their ID as well as the purpose of their travel. They asked me a couple of questions about Vep, my destination, to be sure that I was really from there since I told them that I was on my way to visit my parents. One question was whether Vep had electricity or not. They accepted my "No, it does not, but it's coming soon" for an answer, took a cursory look at my ID book then pressed on.

CHAPTER IV

Near the Railroad Station in the Village of Vep, Hungary
Wednesday, July 11, 1956 1500 Hour

TEN YEARS EARLIER IN 1946, A YEAR AFTER WWII, MY FATHER AND I DUG A HOLE BEHIND A BEE SHACK AT OUR HOME IN VEP AND BURIED AN AUTOMATIC HANDGUN OF SECOND WORLD WAR VINTAGE. I believe it was a Czech made Zbrojovka. As I remembered, it had a fully loaded magazine with seven, maybe eight bullets.

The only problem was that for me Vep was the last place I wanted to be seen. After all, as far as I knew, I was a hunted man.

Most people in the village knew me, including the folks of my old, now ex-friend and a potential hunter in the deadly game, Julius. I believed that if anyone in his family recognized me in Vep, there could be instant communication to Julius, a high-ranking officer in the AVO in Szombathely, only five miles away.

The distance to the railroad station from my parents' home was about two miles. In my high school days—the school was called a gymnasium—an eight-year long middle-school, walking those two miles throughout the nine months of the school was an ordeal. From home to the railroad station, then a twenty-minute train-ride to Szombathely, then to the school from the railroad station, then in the afternoon, from the school to the train and back to Vep, and finally again those two miles. It was a soul-tearing walk. Rain, snow, scorching heat, it was all the same: two miles to walk.

I got off the train early Wednesday afternoon. Not far from the railroad station there was a knoll with willow trees surrounding a small pond. There was no use to go home yet. It was too early. The village was small; it lagged behind the time curve. About three thousand people lived there and everyone knew everybody else, friends and foes alike. I had my share of both. The Communist Party, after a short period of rudderless hesitation, solidified its power at every level of every community in every part of the land. First they polarized the populace, developed an uncanny ability to swing people around like leaves in the autumn wind. Sometimes turning foes to friends, but more often turning friends to foes.

Julius was my childhood friend. We were almost inseparable for years. Then as the years came and went, the distance grew between us. The last I heard, he had a meteor-like career in the AVO. Maybe by now he was even the head of the Szombathely division of that political terror organization… who knows?

Yeah, Julius, I mused.

Now my nemesis. His parent's house was on the way to the railroad station. The guestroom of the house, also called the "holiday room," usually faced the street. The window frame of their guestroom was freshly painted green in 1944, strangely at the same time, when the Hungarian Nazis were moving into power with their arrow cross being green. Sometimes on a black background other times on red maybe white, but the arrow cross always green. Bright green. Now a decade later I still remembered the Nazis, never liked them. They walked in high black boots, black leather jackets, big sidearm pistols. They moved in groups of twos, looking for Jews who were maybe hiding. To me it was rather stupid. Only a few Jewish families lived in the village; one owned a small general store, but disappeared back in '43, God knows where to. The Nazis were telling kids horror stories, warning them to be on guard at all times, for the Jews are godless, they help the Bolsheviks, and they grind up little Christian boys for breakfast, or make them into sausage or soap. So, if one shows up or is found to be hiding, better report him. Some kids were duly frightened, but by the time the hordes of Stalin were pouring over the Carpathian Mountains into the flatlands of Hungary, most of the "kid-eating Jews" were already packed into boxcars, rolling to Auschwitz, and the window frames of Julius' house were painted green. But that was a dozen years ago, so I wondered, *maybe the color is red this time around.*

Times change, window frame colors change, what about people?

To be sure, I'll take a look, I promised myself.

Passing by their house was still some time away. I decided not to show up in the village during daylight. I've got two more days to survive. I had to stay around the railroad station without being noticed 'til darkness came, still hours away. There was ample time that I could spend remembering better days from the past, maybe contemplating the darkness of the future.

I thought of my dad, he worked for the Hungarian State Railroad System for 37 years, never missing a day, as he used to tell with pride. Working for the railroad was the ultimate safe job. During the depression the railroad would not fire people, would not throw them out onto the street, while other companies did. Then came the big war, soldiers had to be transported into the front line, and the railroad became an essential component of the war, workers were needed again. The years were the early forties, the trains headed east, transporting hundreds of thousands of Hungarian soldiers into mass graves on the Ukrainian steppes, in the name of saving Christianity and Western civilization.

The railroad was a way of life. There was free travel on trains for every member of the family, a new uniform every three years for my dad, and medical coverage when needed, although people did not have the habit or the luxury to get sick too often. When they did, they usually died.

***

I was sitting under the shade of a willow tree and something seemed to bother me. Too many demons were floating in and out of my mind, but one bothered me more than the rest.

Which demon was it? That this will be the last time I ever see my parents?

The only two people I loved besides my newly married wife. *What will happen to them? Is that what bothered me? Or was it that the trip may have been in vain if I can't find the gun?*

In the early planning stages George and I assumed that it would take no more than three seconds for a trained person to pull a gun, load it (unless it was already loaded, then reduce the time to two seconds) fire it, and end our dream as well as our life. So in those crucial two or three seconds, ten passengers had to be "neutralized" and one of them, the AVO agent, disarmed. Casualties during the disarming process, including casualties to our team had to be considered. And no matter what else might happen, George's life had to be spared.

He was the only one who knew how to fly.

So for the rest of us, the remaining six, it was imperative to develop a strategic seating arrangement. Each of us needed to sit in a position that would put us in direct proximity to at least two passengers, for each of us had to knock out those two passengers within the critical two or three seconds. We also decided to carry some sort of "weapons" with us, such as a rubber hose-covered lead pipe, billy club, pipe wrench, anything that could be concealed in our carry-on bags. According to the plan, once all the passengers were knocked unconscious, I would be in charge of a quick search for weapons. When the search turned up the agent's gun, I was to seize it, hand it to George, who in turn would knock on the cockpit door. When a crewmember opened the door, George, with gun in hand, followed by Bolla and Charlie, would burst into the cockpit, disarm the crew in the unlikely case they were armed, take over the controls, change the course of the flight, head for the Iron Curtain, fly over Austria, and then on to West Germany occupied by the US Armed Forces. Upon landing, we would ask for political asylum.

The most feared yet hoped-for day in my life was approaching a lot faster than I wanted. The closer it got, the more impossible it appeared.

I realized that the "it" does not even have a name.

Would "stealing an airplane" be the right term?

Maybe, maybe not.

Stealing was a bit of a worn-out and meaningless expression in Hungary in 1956, not even a shameful word anymore. The Almighty State forced thievery to become a way of life, a way of survival. Working for the State, like everyone had to, did not make life a pleasant proposition. Trying to get more goods in exchange for one's productivity became a crime itself. So the next best thing one could do was to steal. Steal anything but most importantly the oh-so-precious commodity, time.

As self-defeating a proposition it may have sounded; like stealing two to three hours of the eight-to-ten-hour workday the State required, may not have given anything except the weird satisfaction of screwing the "Almighty". *You screw us, we screw you.*

I had an analytical mind, but sometimes my target was out of focus; wondering if that was happening now, a way to avoid facing the magnitude of the issue: life or death. In my mind, every plan, no matter how insignificant, had to have three elements: simplicity, purity and balance.

Like music.

"Is there more than one AVO man in disguise, are the pilots armed or both?" I asked George one day. George, as usual, seemed to be hesitant to give a straight answer, at least not immediately.

"I used to steal these things regularly, right?" he said with a question mark at the end of the unfinished and sarcastic sentence, "but damned if I can remember now!"

So that settled it, at least for the sake of any continued conversation. Otherwise it was an ever-larger looming issue, a matter of GO/NO GO as far as I was concerned. But then George came up with Robert and the seven guns. Just like in the fairy tale of Snow White with her seven dwarves, the *Seven Little Helpers*.

I could just see them: cold steel barrel, unforgiving. The guns actually brought one of the three elements of success into play, that of simplicity. You've got seven thieves, for the lack of a better word, differing from the remaining passengers, having a totally different destination in mind, enforceable only by the Seven Little Helpers. Plain and simple!

To escape from a country, to leave the perpetual darkness of days where the sun never seemed to rise, where brutality and inhumanity competed with each other and the combination of those loomed over the land as a slowly descending black blanket… it was no crime to leave.

Immeasurably brutal crimes were committed against humanity by an organized gang of thugs, called the People's Republic of Hungary, their continued existence sanctioned on one side by the T34 tanks of the Soviets and on the other side by the consenting silence of the West.

To me no price was too high in order to get out of this country.

The closer the fateful day approached, concerns about the moral issue kept surfacing with increasing frequency in my mind. The issue of the force we were to use.

To leave the country by escaping was not a moral issue. But using force and endangering the lives of innocent people, was. How much force?

According to the plan using Robert's guns, no force was needed. The guns may never even have to be used. The worst scenario imaginable was that the AVO man would have to be taken out, had he decided to use his gun against the overwhelming firepower of the Seven Little Helpers. Not a real loss, I thought, for the Hungarian AVO was probably one of the most hated terror organizations on Earth.

Still, I tried to banish the thought of killing anyone. I felt reassured that staring into the barrels of seven handguns would make even the most powerful man think twice before pulling the trigger.

Inevitably the image of the "Seven Little Helpers" kept sneaking back into my mind.

Why was George pulling the mysterious Robert and the even more mysterious seven guns, on us? I kept asking myself, but could not come up with an answer.

Doesn't matter anymore, does it? What about the AVO agent? What if there is more than one of them? What about the crew? How many? Are they armed? What about George? Why do I trust him? The question surfaced its ugly face. *What do I know about him? What if he is part of a plot, an AVO undercover?*

On the other hand maybe I should be grateful: he needed to keep the team together, desertion was looming and it would have been deadly. If he invented Robert as a ploy, it certainly worked.

Paranoia kept coming back.

Just how long have I known him…a month, maybe two?

What about my parents? What will happen to them? The Almighty State has no mercy, never had.

My thoughts went back to George, back to the night before. I was now trying to remember telltale signs, like body language, a small clue, but could not remember any. Obviously, I was not paying attention when I should have.

The plan we adopted was a makeshift one. Without guns everything has changed, all of the essential elements vanished. Instead of being in full control of the situation, now the takeover of the aircraft came to the use of sheer, brute force to succeed.

Let's see, I counted to myself. *What if the plane is full? That's 17 people. Seven of us would leave ten of "them", that is, if George is really one of us. But what if he is not? Perish the thought!*

"That leaves ten potential AVO agents and a potentially armed crew of four", I said last night.

"Against the seven of us," added Charlie.

"Make it six," I interrupted, still caressing Anais' beautiful face with my stare.

"By the way," asked Charlie, "how long will it take the AVO guy to pull his gun?" He was asking George. Time now became obviously a major factor.

"Yeah, how long?" Bolla was chiming in.

George responded: "Between two and three seconds."

"So," said Bolla, "we need to knock out ten people. One person in two seconds, roughly."

I was thinking. Knocking ten people cold, even with the element of surprise factored in, within a couple of seconds, one's got to be a real pro.

And I said so.

Charlie retorted: "Have you got a better plan?"

I wish I did, but I had none. So the brute plan of last night had become THE FINAL PLAN.

"And just how do you control your chop-chop without killing some of them?" I asked the by now meaningless question.

"It's kind of late to worry about that," said George.

Nobody disagreed.

Seating arrangements on the plane became another major issue.

Obviously all seven of us could not sit in one group in the same section of the plane, not unless we wanted to whack each other. A floor plan of the DC-3 was produced by George; key seats to be occupied by our team members were identified, numbered and assigned. We knew that there were no attendants on the plane, just the crew and the AVO. No reserved seats either. So we had to board the plane before the rest of the passengers in order to occupy the assigned seats.

"The subjects must be within arm's reach." Bolla announced the obvious.

Timing, surprise, seating arrangements and brute force, that's what had become of our well-structured, meticulously prepared plan overnight.

But halfway through the long night, I made a decision to get a gun, which in turn became the reason for getting off the train at Vep on this Wednesday, July 11, early afternoon.

***

Dogs in the village appeared, at least to the casual observer, outcasts. They were never allowed into the house, not even during the cruelest of winters. When the snow was knee-high the thought was "any dog could wade through that". When the snow got heavier and came up, say, chest-height of a man, the doghouse had to be cleared of snow.

Dogs, while never pampered, were kept in high regards and were considered part of the family. Their main job was to guard the members of the family and their property. Other than depending on their food, they were completely self-reliant. Their food was the leftovers from the kitchen. There was no such thing as "dog-food". If the meal was good enough for the family, well, it certainly was good enough for the dog. And if a dog got sick, nature took its magical course: they either healed on their own or died unceremoniously.

Our dog, Rajna, was no different.

She was about eight years old and maybe the third or fourth in succession of the German Shepherds our family had, all females, succeeding one-another. Her mother died too early for her age, she was no more than five years old—shot by a drunken Russian soldier when she got too threateningly close to him. The dogs in the village hated the uniformed Russians, as if they knew who they were.

The new Rajna (we had to get her from the neighbor who fortunately had an extra pooch still alive) inherited the name, the doghouse, and the unassuming kindness of the family. Almost every household in the village had a dog. On spring nights, when the moon had a round face looking like big cheese in the dark velvet sky, and the air was rich and loaded heavily with the scent of the blooming acacia trees, one could hear the endless howling of the dogs filling the night looking for mating partners.

My father used to say: "Oh Lord, no more dogs!"

No one in the village could afford more than one or at the most maybe two dogs. But when it was time for puppies to come to this world, they were popping out by a half-dozen at a time. So the puppies, except one, maybe two the most, one by one had to be gotten rid of by any means necessary: not a pleasant scene.

I walked through the street gate: it was always unlocked. Rajna greeted me, first with a low growl then as she recognized me, with the greeting that was always the same no matter how much time had passed since the last one. She rubbed herself against my legs and licked my hand.

I patted her head; Rajna was a true friend even though I had not seen her for a long time. In my late teens, a half-dozen years or so ago, there were times when I felt that she was the only friend I had.

The heaviness of the evening was the climax of the long afternoon I had spent near the railroad station, hoping that it would never end. I was afraid of the night coming. The night brought darkness along with the demons.

But now I no longer seemed to have the strength to fight them, the night was their empire. *The demons were the truth* I had come to conclude in the long afternoon.

I needed to retrieve the gun, a vital component of our escape. That's what I made myself to believe. In truth, however, there was another, a much deeper meaning for my visit to Vep. I needed to see them, my beloved parents one more time. There was no question in my mind that after this visit I would never see them again, whether we succeeded or failed with our plan.

But why would I want to see them?

To begin with, I couldn't tell them the truth. Not knowing what I am planning to do would offer them that miniscule chance, perhaps their only chance to survive the onslaught of the terror that would be unleashed upon them by the AVO in two or three days, regardless of what happens Friday.

Now, after my long journey, I couldn't bring myself to go into the house yet. The yard was dark and the silence was deep and frightening. I sat down on a small bench under the huge walnut tree that dominated the yard. Rajna was sitting next to me on the ground. Her head was slightly tilted to the right, full attention in her eyes glowing in the dark. She became part of the silence.

"What am I doing here, Rajna?"

I touched her nose. It was cold and wet, the symptoms of health. She tilted her head the other way now. I knew the answer.

"I am here to trade their lives for my freedom." The cold brutality of the truth was invading me fully.

"I don't have that right, do I, Rajna?" Another head tilt, as if saying: "*Then why are you doing it?*"

Throwing two of the most wonderful, kindest human beings into the cage of the brutes, felt like feeding lambs to the lions.

In exchange for what? The elusive, never experienced dream called freedom, if there is such a thing somewhere.

A dream on one side of the equation, cold reality on the other. The tortures by the thugs of the AVO were known to be beyond anyone's wildest imagination.

And I am here to look into the eyes of these two, who—even though I was not their natural child—took me into their lives, into their hearts, making an unconditional commitment to create a happy life for me, and I am here to send them to the gallows.

"*Where did things go wrong, tell me Rajna! Where did I go off track?*" *Was it the audacity of my selfish ego that wanted to be something that was not agreeable to the social order? Who are they to tell me what I need to be? Who am I to rebel, when everybody else submits? How did this happen?* My thoughts were now racing through my head, as uncontrollable as the demons of the night. *Where was I, what did I do—or not do—to let it get this far? Who was responsible for this firestorm? Who started it?*

The more I'd been thinking the clearer the answer came: *The person responsible for all of this was me.*

ME!

It would have been easy to say, I did not see it coming, but I did. It was my country. It was my decision to let the barbarians rise to power, whether I exercised my rights while I had them, or not.

I saw the prisons built. First for the minds, then for the bodies. The insidious disease, Communism, a wolf in sheep's clothing at first, was marching and I allowed myself to march along. I believed in false promises yet I should have known history—tyranny does not start with the gulags and gas chambers—it ends with them.

But I remained silent and hoped that this time it was going to be *different*. I did not yell "FIRE!" when there was still time. Now it was too late; the fire was raging, the fire hydrants were dry, and all the firemen were dead. The road came to an end, nowhere to turn.

The only thing I had left was my immense guilt, and my longing to see my parents one last time.

"Where am I heading now?"

Rajna's head dropped toward the floor, she laid down on the dusty ground and gently put her front paws on my foot. She had no answer.

The search still did not reach bottom, the demons even now wouldn't let go.

Should I save them by betraying my team and abandoning my dream of freedom? Should I turn myself in and give up those six including my wife? Should I beg for mercy in exchange and believe that any promise they give— if they do—will be kept? Or should I just walk down the block, see Julius' father, and let him make his son a hero to the tyrants?

The demons finally broke their silence in my head, and did it with their heavy artillery: *Here is your trade-off, Zak. On one side the lives of the six, including the life of Anais. On the other side the lives of your parents. Solve it, you are the magician, you created it all!*

There was no solution and I knew it. Rajna came off the ground put her paws around my lap: we both knew that it was the final hug.

Suddenly my chest tightened like being squeezed by an invisible vice, getting tighter and tighter. My breathing got shallow, my heart pumped loud and heavy, I could not stand this never before experienced pain.

I stroked her head and walked into the kitchen.

CHAPTER V

Vep, the County of Vas, Hungary
Wednesday, July 11, 1956 2100 Hour

KNEW THAT IT WAS GOING TO BE A LONG NIGHT. My mom went to sleep at about eleven, but Dad and I talked late into the night, past midnight. After saying good night I told him that I was going to stay up for a while. He went to sleep; I started wandering around until ended up behind the now abandoned bee shack.

I started to dig.

In less than an hour, I found the gun.

It was still wrapped in torn, oily rags covered with dirt and rust. Apparently time took its toll. I brought it to the tool shack, found some kerosene, some sandpaper and went to work.

By sunrise all the moving parts of the gun were working. I greased the firing mechanism; it was clocking. The barrel appeared to be undamaged and the top was sliding smoothly back and forth.

The magazine that I thought to be full with eight bullets had only two. I had no recollection as to what happened to the rest of the bullets, but it did not matter anyway.

There was no way of checking whether the bullets were live and would fire or not…

I hid the gun in the tool shack and went to sleep.

***

I woke up the next morning around 10 am and stayed in the house all morning.

My mother went to work early in the kolhoz (the state-owned collective farm) and dad went to see the village's only physician. My father got hit by a railroad car bumper in 1945 across his chest and his health had been deteriorating ever since. He was eventually put on sick leave by the railroad, extending it on and off. He finally ended up with asthma and had difficulty breathing. He was saddened by the failing of his health he always had been proud of his physical strength and posture. He walked tall even in the darkest of times. He used to say: "That way I am closer to my God in heaven."

I was alone in the house.

After a short search I found what I was looking for. A book written by a Russian author, Sholokhov, entitled: *Quiet Flows the Don,* required reading the last year in high school. The book was about six by nine inches in size, hard cover, approximately 600 pages of text, about two inches thick. I found one of my father's used straight edge razors and began to cut gun shaped holes into the center of the book, starting around page 100, all the way to page 500 or so.

Once completed, the Zbrojovka fit into the hole perfectly. I closed the book. No one would ever know how deadly it was.

Unfortunately, not even me.

Dad came home around noon and my mom early in the evening, worn out, dead tired. As the evening came, storm clouds were gathering over the Alps in the western skies. The train, the only one that could take me to Budapest by the morning, was leaving Vep at 8:30 pm, after stopping only for a couple of minutes. It was still daylight in July.

There was nothing I could do about that.

Saying good-bye was tearing me apart. I did not want to go. I was crying inside like I had never cried before. The words came to my lips to tell them how much I loved them, to tell them to look at me for the last time, the very last time. But the words remained frozen on my lips: they never left. The smile was half-frozen on my face, too. The other half was crying.

I embraced my father first and held him for a long, long time. Suddenly I had a strange feeling that it was not even my father I was wrapping my arms around. Instead I was gripped by the same deadly squeeze that got hold of me the night before in the yard talking with Rajna. It felt like being in a vice, squeezed tighter and tighter until I could no longer breathe.

When kissed my mother on her cheek, I felt the salty taste of her tears in my mouth.

They walked me to the gate.

"I'll be back for Christmas," knowing well that I would never see them again. For some reason, maybe because at other times they did not walk me to the gate, or maybe because of the tears rolling down my mother's face, I was sure that they also sensed that this was the last time they were going to see me.

Slowly I walked down the long block. At the end of the street, before turning the corner, I stopped for a moment, looked back. They were still on the street, outside the gate.

The distance seemed infinite; they seemed to be on another planet. It was almost like a mirage from a distant plateau. A tear rolled down my face, I let it run into the collar of my shirt. I walked in a gray haze of sadness, passing Julius' house, I thought I saw the curtain move.

Hmm.

A block or so later, I realized that I forgot to look at the color of the window frame! But it did not really matter anymore.

The die had been cast.

CHAPTER VI

On the train from Szombathely to Budapest
Thursday Night/Friday Morning

THE TRAIN WAS HALF EMPTY. The conductor, an old timer, reminded me of my father whose hugging arms were still felt around me. A bit of a surprise to me, expecting one of the new breed of conductors: a reformed hooker.

A few years back the Communists, claiming to establish a pure and genderless society, recruited hookers into the honorable profession of railroad conductors. The hooking business got a boost: the hookers no longer had to practice their profession in the doorways of Budapest or on the benches of Varosliget, the official park of the capital. Now there was a new place to provide the "hooking" service, the railroad cars, and a new category of customers, passengers interested in a "quickie". After all, each railroad car had two restrooms. After a while, the practice became unmanageable, the party bureaucrat who came up with the bright idea first got demoted, then fired, probably imprisoned, and eventually disappeared.

Like the hooker conductors, although for them it took longer.

This was to be another sleepless night I thought. I had a small sport-bag with my precious Sholokhov book. I put it under my head, and lay down on the hard bench, trying to sleep.

Where will I be tomorrow night? Then, the inevitably evermore, haunting thought surfaced again:

Who is George?

He's got a wife and young baby girl, no more than a year old. Does his wife know anything? George says she doesn't. But give me a break you're going to leave your wife and baby daughter to the mercy of these brutes? Brutes who torture and murder innocent people for a lot less than stealing the very first airliner in history, causing an international embarrassment to the People's Democracy.

"Well, that's the point exactly," George said at the time, "too much international publicity, the whole world will be looking at them; even the Commies don't want to get a bad name for themselves."

And what about me? I asked myself in the next self-interrogatory period. *What about my dad, the person who means the most in my life? What are they going to do to him? Maybe the same theory would apply that keeps George cool? Far too sensational; too much bad publicity to hurt those who remain behind? Or is it just my excuse?*

I tried to get some sleep but my thoughts were like bees in a beehive, uncontrollably buzzing, allowing no rest for my mind. They kept going back to Vep, then to tomorrow, swinging like a pendulum. My visit was very sad, exceptionally dark and depressing.

There was something about the darkness, more than the lack of electricity combined with the shortage of kerosene for the lonely lamp. It was like an uninvited guest that somehow sneaked into the house and then invaded everything, the conversations, our bodies, ultimately our minds, never wanting to leave. I asked my dad about a small mystery. Now I wish that I did not. His answer was a heart-breaking story.

A year and a half ago, around Christmas time I was home for a couple of days. My father was not there and my mother's story about him not being home was a bit suspicious. She said that my dad was away because he accepted a special "a week-long assignment" at the Szombathely railroad station. The story was limping like a three-legged stool with one leg missing. First, as far as I knew, my dad had a job on the Vep railroad station, not in Szombathely. It was a small reciprocity by the railroad for long and faithful service to accommodate his failing health. He was working as a guard at the station loading and unloading small packages, being around as an extra pair of eyes when some major cargo needed to be loaded or unloaded. Second, the railroad was unlikely to have an "assignment" for any length, let alone for a week. Sounded strange, but it was easier to believe than to press further. With the Communists already in full control anything was possible. The promises were no longer needed; time came for the naked truth. Indoctrination began at age six in the first grade of the elementary school. "Reporting your parents is a duty and an honor. Many of them (your parents) are reactionaries trying to bring back capitalist exploitations. Some others might be organized into an imperialist conspiracy aimed at destroying our People's Democracy, your very future. You must report them, their conversations, if they are listening secretly to Radio Free Europe or Voice of America, so that the Party can change their minds by re-educating them," so went the indoctrination. Hitler's Nazi propaganda minister, Goebbels, had been dead for almost a decade, had committed suicide at the end of WWII, but his teachings were still faithfully followed and applied by the Communists, including the classic one: "repeat a lie 'til it becomes believable."

Bread was in short supply in those days. My mother had to get up at dawn to stand in line at the food warehouse. If she went early enough and was lucky, she could buy a loaf of bread. The villagers, with the exception of a few, no longer owned the land, it belonged to the kolhoz, owned by the "collective". Most of the crop was confiscated by the State whether it was grown on the collectively owned land or on a few remaining acres still in private hands. The Party was in control of the food supply, using it as a powerful weapon. All the confiscated wheat from around the surrounding villages was collected and loaded into freight cars at Vep's railroad station.

It was around mid-December, cold rain was falling. My dad was on the job when a few truckloads of wheat arrived, packed into burlap sacks about 40 pounds each. They were to be loaded and shipped away. In the process of loading, one sack broke open spilling its content on to the muddy ground. The workers did not seem to care, walking over the spilled wheat crushing it into the mud. My father's heart broke seeing the waste; to him it was criminal. He asked the supervisor of the loading, head of one of the kolhoz, if he would be allowed to pick up the wheat in the mud, since it was already wasted.

"Sure Uncle Istvan," said the loading supervisor, he knew my dad, "be sure you clean up afterward." My dad did. He scooped up the wheat along with the mud with his own hands, in cold freezing rain. Carefully, every precious kernel, dumping the muddy mix into a couple of heavy duty paper bags—there were plenty of those around the station—and with a proud smile on his face he presented his "treasure" to my mother.

"Honey," he said, "Look what we've got! Wheat for bread for a few weeks!" Rare smiles were abound: they would take the wheat to the kolhoz's mill in exchange for flour. Of course, first they had to clean up the muddy mess. My dad fashioned a sieve with a small gauge screen. They were washing, cleaning then drying the precious wheat, getting it ready to be exchanged.

The wheat never made it to the mill.

Two days after my dad collected the wheat with the permission of the kolhoz supervisor, two policemen showed up at our home with a warrant in hand *"Stealing property of the People's Republic"* the warrant said. The older of the two policemen was genuinely disgusted with the "rotten job" of arresting my dad; he had known him for a long time and respected his impeccable honesty and integrity. But a job is a job, the warrant was not his decision and he apologized. The other one was a younger cop full of enthusiasm for the job, on his way up, maybe someday a police chief. Anxious to put the handcuffs on my dad's hands until the older one nixed it. My dad walked with them to the police station where a van from the district police headquarters was waiting for him. He was shoved into the police car and taken to Szombathely. His case was presented to a judge by a prosecutor asking for a year imprisonment for the crime committed against the "interest and welfare of the State." The judge heard the prosecutor's harangue for ten minutes then sentenced my dad to one month in prison. He spent that year's Christmas in jail. The story, the third missing leg of the proverbial stool, was told in a breaking voice, choked by emotion and embarrassing tears.

My thoughts had made me tired; must have fallen asleep. I thought I heard George's crackling low voice:

Ladies and Gentlemen! This is your new Captain speaking. I am announcing a small change in the flight plan: we decided to skip Szombathely. We are going on a little longer trip. We'll inform you when we are ready to land in Munich, West Germany. In the meantime, enjoy your flight. It's free!

The dream had disappeared; I woke up. The train had just pulled into the Eastern Station of Budapest.

It was July 13, Friday.

THE LAST HOURS

CHAPTER VII

Budapest, Hungary
Friday, July, 13, 1956 0900 Hour

THE TRAIN ARRIVED ABOUT SEVEN O'CLOCK IN THE MORNING COMING THROUGH THE LONGER ROUTE FROM SZOMBATHELY TO BUDAPEST, TAKING LONG BREAKS AT INTERIM STATIONS, AT GYOR SPECIFICALLY LONGER. Gyor was a major connection station for other trains serving local routes. After arriving at Budapest I hung around Eastern station, looking for a public phone that was operational. I couldn't find one. I walked toward the center of Pest, Deak Square, still looking for a public phone.

I stood on the square; it was rather early for stores to be open. I assumed that the coffee shop on Vorosmarty Square, where the team was to meet and board the bus to the airport, was not open yet either.

Finally, I spotted a phone booth. Someone was standing inside, talking.

A working public phone, hurrah! Long live Socialism! I thought while standing near the booth. Most public phones in Hungary—there weren't many—were permanently out of order. I started walking up and down in front of the booth, making sure that the man inside had noticed me. He did, but did not seem to care. He was chatting endlessly.

I considered the situation. I have to use the phone soon, needed to know how Anais was doing. I could pull the son-of-a-bitch out of the booth. He did not seem to be much of a physical challenge, on the other hand, it may cause a commotion with cops and all, and that was the absolute last thing I needed.

Can I afford it? Hardly. So stay calm.

Finally he hung up the receiver and walked out of the booth.

I could not help it; I was on the edge:

"Jerk!"

He heard it for sure, but ignored me and walked away.

I dialed the phone number of the small hotel where Anais was hopefully still staying. After what seemed to be forever, a man answered.

"Yeah?"

"Would you get me Anais, please!"

"Who?"

Oh, not again, I thought, *I shouldn't have called her by name.*

That was the deal, arranged by the assistant manager who was Charlie's friend. Charlie had arranged to register us without using our ID Book. No small feat, because by now the Communists were able to exercise tight control over everyone's identity. The identity document, the "ID Book", was a passport resembling identification book that every person in Hungary, regardless of age, had to have in his/her possession. You could be stopped on the street, in a store, at a railroad station by the AVO, State Security, military personnel, or street cops and be demanded to show your ID Book. That ID Book (for the Party members the book was red) had to have information indicating where you lived, stayed, resided, or worked. Unemployed in the Socialist State was considered vagrancy, regarded and could be punished as a felony.

Trying to live in Budapest was especially tough.

The Communists did not want people from the countryside to congregate in Budapest looking for jobs. Consequently, you either had a legal, verifiable residence in Budapest or had a police stamped permit allowing you to stay there beyond 24 hours.

"I mean the woman in room 313…sorry," I corrected myself on the phone accordingly to our previous understanding. A nerve-racking long silence ensued, but finally she was on the phone.

"Oh my God," she said.

I hoped that the clerk did not hear that. Referring to a nonexistent, strictly barred entity named God was not a very smart thing to say in Hungary.

I should mention that when I see her.

Then again, I thought, *Why?* If we were not going to make it, as it seemed likely to me, we'll see Him in person in short order, maybe even before the day is out, so no use denying Him. On the other hand, if by whatever miracle, we end up in the free world, outside of this forlorn, hopelessly devastated country, the belief in God's existence is, if not accepted, at least tolerated.

"See you at eleven," I said and hung up.

I still had a little money left in my pocket and remembered that we had "weapons" to buy. On one of the side streets, they were reaching out of Deak Square like arms of a mechanical octopus. I finally found a hardware store in the process of opening. A tall guy in light blue overalls was just finishing the rolling-up of the corrugated aluminum door panels as I walked in, looking for a pipe wrench, although I doubted that I had enough money to buy one.

Let's try anyway.

The clerk came around; ever so helpful.

"We've got some with screwed-up threads," he said when I started to bargain. Then he looked around as if ready to reveal a secret, but first examining the walls for maybe having ears, when continued.

"You know, a Socialist competition product, I mean…" Then winked his eye and swallowed the rest of the sentence.

"Cheaper, reduced, almost free, you know, say how about half price?"

Another true believer, I thought with irony.

"I'll take the wrench," I told him. He charged me about a third of what the price tag said.

On the outside I doubled back on the other side of the street, watched the door of the hardware store for a while.

Plain paranoia.

The coffee shop on Vorosmarty Square was open by the time I arrived. Instead of entering I walked around the square stealing a glance here and there, looking at times straight forward, looked in the reflection of the windows for shadows of imaginary predators.

Where will they apprehend us if they know? I wondered.

Did someone give up the plan? Was George a set-up? Should I walk away, go into some hiding place, just to save my life? But where to?

Fear, like a huge black monster, was hovering over Vorosmarty Square with its tentacles firmly rooted in every street corner. Now it slowly lowered its humongous, ugly body, full of warts on its belly, onto the square. The daylight was beginning to darken, almost as if the sun had never came up.

I had to escape this vision. The image of darkening skies in the middle of the day was inhibiting my breathing process, shortening my inhale and exhale, driving up my heartbeat, it was choking me.

***

When I walked into the coffee shop, it was close to eleven o'clock. The bus to the airport was to leave at 11:45 am.

The team was there.

Charlie was treating everyone, spending money like a drunken sailor. His folks had money. Charlie also had a watch; as a matter of fact, he was the only one in the group who had a watch. He took it off, ceremoniously handed it to George.

"The pilot," he announced loudly, "has to have a watch!"

"Cool it, stupid!" whispered Bolla, looking around.

Charlie opened his mouth, ready for a comeback. Then he looked at George and knew that it was time to shut up. I sat down between Anais, who had just arrived, and George. Then I took my precious Sholokhov book and laid it on the table, creating curious looks from everyone in the group.

"Required reading for George," I said and pushed the book across to my left in front of him. As George reached for the book, I laid my hand on the cover, preventing it from being open.

"A very careful reading," I emphasized.

I felt a muscle twitching in George's hand as it brushed over my own. My hand was still resting on top of the book. I knew he'd gotten the message.

"I see," said George. Then he slid the book in front of him without opening it.

After a while he got up, looked around for a restroom, spotted the sign and walked away with the book under his arm. He came back a few minutes later, sat down and said casually:

"Interesting reading for the trip." Then he turned to me.

"Kind of a short reading though, isn't?"

I agreed. I knew he was referring to the shortage of bullets.

An exhibition boxing match was scheduled for that evening in Szombathely that I had arranged for, in case we needed a cover for the unusual way of heading to Szombathely. The "excuse" of flying commercial was, if needed, that we missed the train so we had to take the plane in order to get there in time. It could be a real, legitimate cover on the surface. However, we would be hard pressed to explain some of the contents of the carry-on bags should they be searched, let alone the fact that our tickets were purchased a couple of days before.

I looked at Anais and saw dark circles drawn around her eyes. For all of her twenty years, she looked like an old woman.

***

During the days of preparation for the escape an important question arose: would we want to look like a real boxing team on our way to an exhibition match or as individuals not even knowing one another? Would we want to deal with the potential inquiries that could be triggered by the dangling boxing gloves attached to our sport bags? Those questions could be deadly especially if they were penetrating beyond the thin surface of the lies.

Or do we want to fly as regular passengers, seven most unlikely passengers, flying on a Communist Hungarian domestic airline frequented by Party functionaries or company executives—usually being one and the same—but definitely different in appearance, older and a lot more businesslike than us?

Which way is safer?

Or, which way is less revealing?

The final decision went against the boxing team appearance version, against the dangling boxing gloves. Accordingly, each of us was to be on our own. It meant that every one of us would have to handle our own airline tickets.

It was 11:30 am when the airport shuttle arrived it was time to board and face the next stage of our journey.

"Check your tickets" said George, and added, "Until we land, this is your chance to say goodbye to one another!"

He sounded ominously somber, maybe the first time I heard George sounding like that. Actually it was the first time that the magnitude of what was really happening sank in with its full weight, numbing my mind.

I turned to Anais.

"I love you, I always will, even in my death."

She smiled when she said:

"Oh no, we won't die. Not for a while."

Her moist eyes made me wonder what exactly she meant by *for a while.*

***

The Ferihegy Airport was the "hub" for all domestic air traffic in Hungary—five round-trips daily—only one heading in the westerly direction. There were few international flights with a special boarding area controlled by the AVO.

As we were getting off the shuttle bus, a uniformed officer broke the passenger group into two sections. I was in the second group. The first group was led into the building while we were standing around on the sidewalk. Long minutes passed. Finally, another uniformed person came out of the building and allowed us to proceed inside.

The lobby was relatively busy. There were about twenty people standing around, including passengers I remembered seeing on the bus. I spotted only Charlie, Joe and Gabor of our team, they were in the second group. I looked at the clock on the lobby's wall; it was 1:57 pm. Three minutes to scheduled departure time.

Where were George, Bolla and Anais?

***

A uniformed person stepped up to the door and stood there for what seemed to be a long time before he announced:

"Rest of the passengers for HA-LIG. Line up here please!" He was pointing toward the door.

So the other members of the team are already on the plane, I assumed with slight relief.

Seven passengers were lining up, including four from our team. I could not get to the front of the line. I settled for third place, with two "real passengers" ahead of me and three of my teammates behind me. The uniformed guy started checking the tickets. He took mine, looked at it then looked at me.

Nerve-wracking moments. He looked at the ticket again.

Maybe he is contemplating a question. What would that be? And what would my answer be?

"Szombathely?" he asked the obvious and totally unnecessary question.

"All the way," I said, forcing a smile.

He looked at me one more time:

"Have a good trip!" and handed it to me.

He checked the rest of the tickets, then stepped to the head of the line, opened the door and led us to the plane. We had to walk around the back of the plane; the boarding was on the far side of the DC-3.

I was able to pass one passenger ahead of me, but when I tried to squeeze by the other, he grumbled at me.

"What's your hurry, the plane won't leave without you!"

I wish I could tell you bud, but maybe I will in Munich what my hurry was all about, I thought and got on the plane behind him.

After climbing the stairs, I looked around the cabin.

This is it then, I thought, *the chariot to freedom, or a flying coffin to death.*

CHAPTER VIII

Ferihegy Airport - Budapest, Hungary
Friday, July 13, 1956 1410 Hour

THE LEFT ENGINE KICKED IN FIRST. The huge propeller started spinning, the blades turned into a magical transparent disc. The back of the engine spat out a black cloud of smoke that first turned white, then thinned out and eventually disappeared. Less than a minute later the right engine fired up and soon they were running in rhythm. The Captain, apparently satisfied that the aircraft was in the clear, took the breaks off. The DC-3 shuddered reluctantly then began to roll on the tarmac, taxiing for takeoff.

Destiny was on its unpredictable way.

We were heading toward the end of the runway. I thought it was time to take inventory of the occupants in the passenger cabin, when the plane slowed down.

No reason for that, was there? Being a novice of air travel, panic did not set in immediately. But it did hit me with full force when the DC-3

53

ground to a full stop. I looked out the porthole-sized window on my left and what I saw was ready to stop my heart.

A small white van with its emergency lights turned on raced toward the plane. I could hear the wailing of the siren as it approached.

That's it! We're doomed! One of us must've let the AVO know about our plan. The van probably has a contingency of AVO agents ready to arrest us. What to do now?

Yell to George?

But what if George is part of the plot? Maybe he planned it all along from the beginning. Maybe that's the way he planned to get back to his dreams, flying jets in the Air Force.

But why did they drag it out this far? Just giving enough rope to hang ourselves? Obtaining enough evidence to corner us? Why? The Communist justice does not need foolproof evidence to convict, why the long leash?

Maybe I am accusing George unfairly. He might be as much of a victim as all of us and probably he'll be hung right next to me.

What to do?

Does George see what I see? Is he going to make a move? Should I go and tell him to start the takeover while still on the ground, and maybe risk the whole plan? Can they stop the aircraft from taking off by driving their truck in front of it?

Now the van must have arrived: the siren sounded right next to the plane on the door side and then it stopped. The pilots must have cut back on the power. The spinning of the blades seemed to be slowed down, so did the sound of the engines.

The increasing silence was eerie.

***

My legs trembled as I was about to rise and move up the aisle to talk to George, but my feet refused to take orders from my brain. In the midst of this fearful hesitation, the cockpit door opened. A uniformed man stepped out, leaving the door slightly ajar. He wore a white shirt with a few narrow black bars on its shoulders. I thought he must be the pilot, maybe the co-pilot and if he was, what was he doing in the passenger cabin?

He walked down the aisle to the outside door, right across from my seat. He stopped, reached for a red-colored metal bar, pulled it down, and opened the door.

What will happen now?

The van was parked next to the plane with its siren now silent. The man in uniform leaned out of the plane. Way out. I thought he might even fall, but he did not. Instead, he leaned back into the plane, clutching a large, gray canvas bag with a padlock on. He swung the bag and threw it right behind my seat next to some wooden crates. Still holding on to the fuselage, he reached out again, pulled another bag in, and threw that one behind my seat as well. Then he yanked the door shut and pushed the red lever down. The latch, snapped hard into place, closed again.

Are we safe now? I asked myself.

The man moved toward the cockpit, mumbled half-aloud, almost apologizing.

"They are pulling this late mail delivery shit every time when Edo is doing the mail. How many times have we told him that we won't stop the next time?" Then he walked into the cockpit and shut the door, this time for good.

My heart almost regained its normal rhythm now.

We are safe! We are safe! Pounded my heartbeat.

Until when? The demons came laughing.

The DC-3 rolled again, this time all the way to the end of the taxiway. It did a ninety-degree turn and lined up with the runway. The pilots powered up the engines, props became spinning discs again, and thirty seconds later HA-LIG Flight 387, rising like a huge albatross, left the ground and a new chapter in the history of aviation was soon to be written.

ON BOARD TO
FREEDOM OR DEATH

CHAPTER IX

Aboard HA-LIG Flight 387
Airspace of Szil, 95 Km west of Budapest, Hungary
Friday July 13, 1956 Around 1430 Hour

EORGE WAS THE CAPTAIN OF OUR TEAM. The plan, with details worked out three nights earlier, finally went like this: exactly five minutes before the takeover fight was to start, George will give a signal to start the countdown to the takeover. He would get up from his seat, lean across of the aisle toward the windows on the opposite side, announcing aloud:

"Look, there's Gyor!"

Gyor was the fourth largest city in Hungary, en route to Szombathely, about eight miles away from the flight path. It would be clearly visible from the left side of the aircraft.

George was to make this particular announcement to coordinate our action. Since he was the only one with a watch, he knew where ground zero for the countdown would be. Gyor was at a critical point of the flight in our plan: five minutes after leaving the airspace of

Gyor, which was actually called Szil airspace, the crew would be first reporting to ground control, entering Szombathely airport's landing approach about 15 minutes later. So, when George was going to get up, according to the plan, everyone would start the countdown to coordinate our actions.

The countdown—actually it should have been called a "count-up" was to start at 100 and end at 400, a count of 300, exactly five minutes. When the countdown reached 400 we were to make our move.

The DC-3 had two rows of seats, a single row on each side of the aisle with two bulkhead seats next to the cockpit door facing backwards. The door to the outside, the boarding/exit door, was at the right hand side across from my seat. The DC-3 was a converted C-47 licensed to the Russians who then built over four thousands of them under the code name of Li-2 (The design engineer's name was Lisunov) and it had seventeen seats. The stairs were built into the door.

Another step closer, I thought, as I was looking over the passenger cabin to see just how badly the critical seating arrangement got screwed up. The passengers settled in comfortably for a flight scheduled to last an hour. It was time to take inventory, a passenger inventory, that is. There were three empty seats, which meant fourteen passengers: seven of us and seven of "them" the real passengers including the AVO agent.

Which one?

I stood for a while trying to get a better view of the cabin. The passengers were hardly visible; my view was obstructed by the tall backs of the seats. I started my analysis of what I could see on the port side of the isle.

At the cockpit door facing backwards, a bulkhead seat was occupied by a short man in his early thirties, a potential AVO agent. He was wearing a dress suit, no tie, revealing an open-neck shirt. His head was slightly balding he acted with great familiarity making his presence obvious to everyone.

Just a bit too obvious, I thought.

Facing him sat a woman. No suspect at all; the AVO would not trust a woman with a gun.

The next passenger in seat number three looked like a bureaucrat with heavy horn-rimmed glasses wearing a business suit. I dismissed him as another unlikely suspect. In seat number four sat Bolla, our heavyweight. Other than him, I was the only team member sitting on the port side of the cabin. Between his seat and mine there were three more seats, all occupied by real passengers. Not very good news as far as our pre-arranged seating plan was concerned.

Later we learned what interrupted our seating arrangement plan.

At boarding time, a uniformed airline employee led seven people to board, including George, Anais and Bolla from our team and four "real passengers" who occupied the left of the aisle seats along with Bolla. Then the ground crew interrupted the boarding process, allowing a small forklift to drive up to the plane to unload three wooden crates with aluminum cables wrapped inside, cargo. The crates were stacked up in the back end of the aisle before the other seven passengers, including me and three other team members were led to the plane for boarding. When I got aboard, the only empty seats on the left side were seats number eight and nine. Seven was already occupied; I took number eight while seat nine remained empty. As I took a closer look at those three authentic passengers on the port side, I was convinced that the AVO agent was amongst them.

But again, which one?

I was not going to be able to knock out three people, two of them relatively well built, not within three seconds. So I had to establish my priorities. The one right in front of me looked "promising." *What a way to look at your future victim.* Short, military-looking haircut, wide shoulders, mid-thirties. I noticed that he took a scanning, almost appraising look of the cabin.

Maybe I should take it for a telltale sign. Or was it my imagination working overtime?!

On the starboard side, in the bulkhead seat next to the cockpit door, sat George. The seat facing him was empty. *At least he is sitting where he is supposed to,* came a calming thought of small consequence. In seat number three sat Charlie, acting friendly with passengers around him, the usual jovial Charlie. The entire right side of the aisle, with one exception of an authentic passenger, was occupied by our team. Seat number four was Joe, seat number five "real passenger", seat number six Anais, and finally, in seat number seven was Gabor. Then there was an empty space for the doorway to open and another empty seat in the back.

***

The plane reached its cruising altitude around 10,000 feet. The roaring of the engines had quieted into the purr of a cat. When George leaned out of his seat in a rather casual way and called "Gyor", nobody seemed to pay attention.

Except six passengers, for whom at that moment, a countdown of life or death had begun....

THE COUNTDOWN

ONE HUNDRED ONE...
ONE HUNDRED TWO...

THE STRANGEST THING WAS HAPPENING. The cabin became a movie theater. There was a screen up in front and someone in the back was operating a slide projector. The slides were my life...

***

The late Nineteen Twenties in Vep, Hungary.

They called her Etti, short for Etelka. She was the fourth of ten children; all had been registered on their birth certificates by their long Christian names. There was a practical reason for the shortened version of their names. Not only would it have been a tongue-twister to pronounce those long names, but just think of the poor mother who had to yell at ten kids with long names. Forget it! So their names were shortened to convenient nicknames: Erzsebet to Erzsi, Kelemen to Kel and so on. Having ten children meant a large family, but not an unusual one. Those big numbers were to forecast caretaking and old-age security since the chances of the parents being supported when they got old were directly related to the number of offspring, and their subsequent accomplishments in life.

Youngsters usually got married in their mid to late twenties and as a rule they remained virgin until the night of the wedding.

There were seven girls, in addition to three boys in the family. With the exception of one girl, Roza, the rest of the girls were not particularly pretty, but being pretty was not a prerequisite for a good marriage.

The family, like most families in Vep, were serfs, working on the large estate of the Erdodys, who had large land holdings and were considered "good" landlords. Not only was there always work for everyone, but the Erdodys were decent and fair in taking care of the members of their serfdom.

The majority of the jobs were for sharecroppers. Not an easy job but life was not supposed to be an easy proposition anyway. If you were a woman, your choices were more limited than if you were a man. A man could always work for the government, become a soldier, a policeman, maybe a tax collector; he might even land a cream-of-the-crop job, working for the railroad.

Etti was lucky. At age 26 she married a railroad man called Istvan. He was two years younger and came from a family of eleven, also serfs for the Erdodys. Istvan "struck gold" during the failed Communist revolution of Bela Kun in 1919. He volunteered to work for the armored railroad division, fighting the Soviet-like Communist insurgency. Eventually the Bolshevik Revolution and the accompanying red terror was successfully destroyed thus ending the short-lived Dictatorship of the Proletariat.

The railroad knew what gratitude was all about and Istvan got a lifetime job. Thus he became a great "catch" for a husband at age 24.

Their wedding was a simple affair. The parents of both Etti's and Istvan's showed up along with Etti's young sister Roza and one of Istvan's younger brothers. It was summertime and harvesting the crop was a lot more important to people in the village than an everyday event like marriage. What really mattered to Istvan and Etti though, was that outside of their parents the most important "person" the only One who really mattered, the Lord Himself, was there, duly represented by the village priest.

It was in His presence, that Istvan, dressed in his freshly washed and ironed railroad uniform firmly said, "Yes, I will," when asked by the priest of his intention of spending the rest of his life with "this woman, Etti".

She was also dressed for the occasion. She wore a frilly white blouse that she washed more than once to get it sparkling white. To her, the purity of the white blouse somehow reflected the purity not only of her intentions, but the life she had lived for 26 years. She was still a virgin, and while a passing pride occupied her mind for a while, she realized that there was nothing to be proud of, that's how it was supposed to be. She did not have a matching skirt to go with the blouse, not even a black one to accentuate the white, so she borrowed a light grey one from her younger sister, Margit. After she muttered an almost inaudible, "Yes, I will," the ceremony shortly came to an end, not only because there was not a lot else to say on that hot July afternoon, but because the priest had to move on as well. There was a funeral a bit later where he had to perform. Etti's mother had one of the young roosters butchered and broiled for the event, and with that dinner, their married life began.

It quickly ran onto difficult tracks; Etti could not get pregnant.

They were sad and confused. To them, God created man and woman and their consequent union for only one purpose: to produce and raise a family. To them, God created sex and thus man and woman differently, not for their joy and pleasure—*oh, no!*—but to keep mankind flourishing and to populate His masterpiece, Earth. They tried for a while, to no avail. They had no idea what to do. It would have been embarrassing to see a doctor; besides, what could a doctor do anyway? On the other hand, being childless could have meant that one of them had done some serious sinning prior to their holy union. When this surfaced as a potential reason, the inevitable question came along, which of them did the sinning? Istvan or Etti? Who was to ask to find out?

They were magnanimous souls so they blamed themselves. They were confessing to each other, as well as to the priest, every sin they could think of regardless of how small and meaningless. Even thinking about a sin was a sin to confess. The priest meted out what seemed to be an appropriate penitence, a dozen rosaries for each separately and a dozen to be said jointly. A couple of days for Istvan to work on the parish property, building a shack for the goat the priest had recently acquired, for Istvan was very good at carpentry.

"How come you don't work for the Erdody's carpentry shop?" asked the priest.

Istvan was nailing in the final board to the shack's doorway and just shook his head.

"I like the railroad," he said, then somehow managed enough courage to ask:

"Reverend, do you think that God will consider our trouble more kindly now?"

"You know, Istvan, I really cannot tell you, but I do know that if you double your prayers, God will double your chances to resolve your problem."

The priest was educated enough to know that the double of zero was still zero, but he was not in the business to deliver math to the parishioners; his job was to dispense hope.

After a while there seemed to be no solution in sight. Their short-lived sex life came to an end.

Now what to do? Divorce?

The word did not even exist in their vocabulary.

The years came and went with the ever-diminishing hopes that God would provide answers in this life. But God was omnipotent and His Ways could be strange and unpredictable. He had the answer. He was just holding it back.

***

The younger sister of Etti, named Roza short for Rozalia, was a strange kid. Instead of working for the Erdody's, she always wanted to go to the "big city", Szombathely. As far as the rest of the family was concerned, only strong men like the male members of the family—Janos, Joska and Ferenc—would be able to survive and repel the sinful temptations of the big city; sins sure were dominant there! All warnings and pleadings were in vain. At past age eighteen, she packed her little bag and walked the five miles to Szombathely.

"She is the black sheep," said Ferenc, the oldest son, the recognized elder and self-appointed spokesman of the family. But Janos, the next in line age-wise, was a bit more condescending:

"Each family has one," he said, offering a lame apology on Roza's behalf.

It was late summer, sometime in September 1930, and the early winds of the impending global depression were already blowing over the Atlantic, heading for Europe. A traveling circus had just arrived in Szombathely, like it did twice a year, to put on a show that lasted four to six days depending on the anticipated attendance. Roza was saving her money to see the show. The ticket was not too expensive; it would come to half of what she saved in a couple of months. She dreamed about seeing the acrobats, dancing elephants, jugglers swallowing swords, the whole incredible world of magic.

At the entrance, the ticket taker was a good looking young man, who, after taking a second look at Roza, flashed a beautiful smile. Roza saw it, but she got embarrassed and turned her head away. She still remembered him—how could she not—when he appeared again, this time as one of the trapeze artists. Death-defying loops, grabbing the swinging bar at the very last fraction of a second brought Roza's heartbeat into overtime. She was scared to death that the young man, who could not be more than 20 years old, would fall and break his legs or arms or, God forbid, get killed. She also realized that there was more to her fears than just worrying about the boy's safety. When the show was over and the small crowd was spilling out into the warm September night, what in Hungary was called the *Summer of Old Women*, there he was again at the exit. Half of Roza's heart wished that he would not see her, but the other half harbored hopes otherwise.

Not only did he notice her, but as she passed by, he reached out for her arm, gently separating her from the passing crowd.

"What's your name, sweetie?"

She was speechless.

"Would you come again tomorrow? I'll be at the gate," he continued, "I'll be taking tickets. I can let you in free! My name is Peter," he added with a smile. His eyes were full of warmth, like that warm late September night. She still did not answer, left with an almost embarrassing smile on her pretty face and went back into the little cubbyhole in the basement of the building where the people for whom she worked, lived.

When she showed up at the circus the next evening, the boy had a huge smile on his face:

"I knew you'd come," he said. His voice lacked arrogance or self-assurance. It was just a voice of a happy boy, she thought. The circus stayed in town for two more days and left late Saturday night. She was crying as he was holding her in his arms before parting and she hardly heard when he said that he'd be back and that they would marry and be happy forever.

"I'll be back in a few months!" he promised.

He never returned.

She was waiting every day. Then finally, six months later, the circus came back. She was way into her pregnancy by then. It looked obvious, undeniable. She went to the circus, hanging on to her fading hopes, maybe she would see him again. When all the people were inside and the show was about to start she walked up to an old man. He was the ticket taker now, closing the canvas door. She softly asked about Peter. At first, the old man ignored her. Then, as he took a second look, this time at her belly, he stopped. He poked his finger toward her belly as his face contorted into a question mark. He did not have to ask, she did not have to answer. She just nodded her head. The question mark on the face of the old man turned into sadness.

"Honey, he fell. A couple of weeks after we left here the last time, he fell. He was such a good boy we all loved him. He was so talented, never wanted to have a safety net. That way people were more thrilled. His artistry pleased the crowd, raised the attendance. Then he fell." He kept repeating himself, trying to hide a tear that was slowly rolling down on his face.

"He fell, lived a few days and then he died. Nothing could be done." The old man just kept murmuring as he was leaving for the inside of the tent, closing the gate. Then he hesitated and turned back; "I could tell you where he is buried."

She did not want to know. She had to go home, a home she no longer had. But still, she just had to see her mother one more time and take the poison that all those unfortunates who wanted to die were taking. She heard that it was a very painful and slow way to die, but the stuff was easy to get; people were using it for rat poison. They called it arsenic or something like that, a very mean poison. Or maybe she should jump in the front of the train, the express one that rolls through Vep without stopping, right around noontime. A real fast and sure way to go.

The shock of the family in Vep was as she expected. There was no bigger shame for the family than a pregnant daughter without a husband. Unthinkable.

The night Roza thought would be her last, Etti was lying in bed with eyes wide open. She knew that Istvan was not asleep either.

"Are you thinking what I am thinking?" she asked. He did not have to answer. It seemed to be God's answer for their sufferings. God, in his Greatness, reached out to them and offered a long-sought answer.

"Just as God is our Father, I'll promise to be that of her child, boy or girl, doesn't matter," Istvan said.

They took Roza into their little home where she stayed inside, out of the sight of the villagers' eyes, and three months later, on June 22, 1931, I was born.

Then she left. Headed back to the big city in search of another job, never to see a circus again. In Vep, the village notary knew Istvan and liked him. While the mother's name had to be registered without naming a father to reflect the unpleasant truth, the notary promised that the documents would be as good as dead, buried deep in the files as long as he stayed in office.

"Joe, my father, you knew him, the notary before me," he said to Istvan, "he died in office in his late seventies. I should have a few more years around here," he laughed as he shook Istvan's hand.

Roza visited my parents and me at least once a year. I had no idea why she always had misty eyes. Nor could I figure out why she always brought small presents when she came.

I was sixteen when I learned the truth: I was a bastard.

The love lavished on me by my adopting parents, Etti and Istvan, was unconditional. I could not figure out why I did not have a brother or a sister, maybe more than one of each, like other families. I finally arrived at a theory that love is something that people have limited amounts of and my parents didn't want to waste any amount on other kids, brothers or sisters.

As I was growing up, I got more attached to my father than to my mom. She was a bit slow and always complained of headaches. But I knew she loved me with all her heart. She was a simple soul, uncomplicated with an almost fanatical faith in God, never ever doubting His Will, the Might and the Eternal Justice of the Lord. She was convinced beyond any doubt that her place in Heaven was already reserved. Beyond the love of God, I meant everything to her. Her life, just like everybody else's was a mosaic of the turbulent times of that era, although in the earlier years a bit more sheltered.

Until the war came.

Etti respected people, all people, because they were created in God's image, and if they were sinning, God was there to forgive. The war and its aftermath, however, changed everything. The brutality of the occupying Russians, then the destruction of everything that was sacred to Etti by the godless Communists had turned a decent life into one of unbearable pain filled with fear and depression.

(The preceding chapter was reconstructed based on lengthy conversations with my biological mother Roza, and with my adopting father, Istvan).

ONE HUNDRED EIGHTEEN...
ONE HUNDRED NINETEEN...

THE FIRST DECADE OF MY LIFE WAS UNEVENTFUL. When I was a year old, my dad was transferred to Celldomolk, a railroad town about 25 miles east of Vep. I attended a Catholic grade school, but missed quite a few school days, as I was often sick. My dad got housing from the railroad, a guardhouse at the crossing of the railroad and the road to three cemeteries of the city: one Catholic, one Protestant and one Jewish. Usually a rough combination for getting along, but once their occupants were dead they tolerated being near to each other rather peacefully. Our housing was free. It was a blessing 'til the depression came, then it became a mixed blessing at best. My earliest recollections of life were those muffled cries of my mother:

"Oh Lord, save his soul!"

I had no idea who the Lord was, what a soul was, but even if did know, I would not have any idea whose soul it could have been. I remembered the solemn haggard look on my father's face as he grabbed a big, empty paper bag used for holding cement, put on his gloves and left the house. For a long time, I had no idea what those heavy gloves were for in the midst of a hot summer. Years later, I learned that the big, heavy duty paper bags were for collecting body parts of people committing suicide by throwing themselves in front of the express train that came through from Budapest around noon every day. Right at the road crossing the railroad tracks in front of the guardhouse we lived. The larger mangled parts of the mutilated bodies - torsos, limbs, head - were picked up by a two-man, hand-driven trailer, rolling on the tracks. My father's assignment was to clean up the remaining mess by picking up the small, scattered leftovers of sad souls who could not handle the earth's miseries anymore. He collected the disheveled small body parts into the cement bag, then handed the bag over to the same railroad people who came back a couple of hours later.

Those were the dark years of the Great Depression.

"Oh Lord save his soul!"

***

When I was ten, my father was transferred again, this time to Karpathorussia, a large territory of Northeast Hungary repatriated after twenty years. The year was 1941, the start of the war between Germany and Russia; Hungary, as usual, got caught in the middle. People of Hungary lived in a blind stupor of a dream, the hopes of the eventual return of the Fatherland. This hope lived ever since 1919, the year when the heads of the winning countries of the First World War, Lloyd George of England, Clemenceau of France, and Woodrow Wilson of the USA, divided Europe at a dinner table at Trianon. In the process of punishing the losers under the pretense of "never to have another war again" they decimated Hungary, carving up its thousand-year-old territory.

Transylvania accounted for half of Hungary's land mass and one third of its natural resources. It was transferred to Rumania virtually with a stroke of a pen in Trianon. The aftermath of the treaty, one of the most brutal genocides of the twentieth century was off and running against the Hungarian populace of Transylvania. The conscience of the League of Nations and the bleeding hearts of the West remained stoically silent. Hungary never seemed to be the favorite of the West. But the people of Hungary were dreaming of the day, when all injustice would end and Hungary would be the same again. Instead came Hitler. He re-divided Europe in the Treaty of Vienna, (1938) returned token areas to Hungary to keep the flame of irredentism alive and to gain alliance of Hungary for the coming war.

Karpathorussia was part of the returned territories and the railroad transferred my father to a town called the House of King in the Carpathian Mountains. We spent less than two years there. By 1943 the Third Reich was running out of steam. The armies of Stalin, from Byelorussians and the Ukrainians all the way to the warriors of the Khazak steppes, were on the march intent to destroy Western Civilization, along the line of the alleged mission of wiping out the Nazi monster, Adolf Hitler, with whom Stalin signed a meaningless non-aggression pact a couple of years earlier. My father was transferred back to Szombathely in 1943. We moved into our little house in Vep that my father built in the late twenties. It had one bedroom, one kitchen, one small pantry; the building was attached to my grandmother's house which was very similar, except it had one extra bedroom, facing the street, used for occasional guests only.

The war inevitably arrived.

School days were cut short. Starting in the fall of 1944 they were shut down entirely. American bombers came flying high above, heading north. Their main target was Wiener-Neustadt, south of Vienna in Austria, where Hitler had one of the factories manufacturing parts for the pride of Luftwaffe, the Messerschmidts, a fighter interceptor plane. In late 1944, the Soviet steamroller got stalled for a while at Budapest;

41,000 Germans and 51,000 Hungarians dug in, holding up the Soviet Army, a force that was well over a hundred thousand strong.

The front stalled for weeks. Stalin was unhappy about the delay.

Dealing with Churchill and Roosevelt in the Yalta Agreement, Stalin got a deal known as "what you occupy is yours". So the race was on and Stalin was out to grab much of Europe, as much as he could. His armies had to march at any cost and march fast. Then this "garbage bunch of gypsies", these "Hungarian mercenaries", were holding up the march of his invincible armies. The commander of the assault on Budapest during the winter of 1944/45 was Marshall Tolbuchin and now his ass was on the line. So he told Stalin that a few hundred thousand Hungarians were holding Budapest. Eventually Budapest fell and Stalin, being the ultimate pragmatist, wanted to know what happened to those few hundred thousand Hungarians that were holding up his armies, costing him those precious territories of Europe.

Where were they?

"Half of them dead and the other half are on the way to the gulags," reported Tolbuchin.

So in the ensuing months, long after the end of the war, a hundred thousand Hungarians between the ages of 15 and 50 were rounded up indiscriminately while walking on the streets and shipped to the gulags as the "captured defenders of Budapest…"

Most of them had never even seen Budapest, let alone defended it.

***

I used to hang out in our backyard with kids from the neighborhood watching the bombers flying by. German anti-aircraft batteries kept shooting at them, but they were flying too high for any accurate hit.

Once in a while there were aerial dogfights, especially when the Americans were heading back south after completing a raid and the German ME109's attacked a wounded bomber or a lonely escort fighter.

Aerial dogfights were fun to watch.

At night the English bombers came raiding. They were dropping flares, what people called "Stalin candles", although they had nothing to do with Stalin, or rather, Stalin had nothing to do with them; to illuminate targets way up north before dropping their deadly payload. My family, along with the neighbors, used to gather in the backyard where a bomb shelter was dug into the ground. But we never had to get into it. Instead, we watched the flares at night and listened to the faraway explosions.

Then on Sunday, March 4, 1945, things dramatically changed.

With my best friend Julius, we biked to Szombathely to play soccer. The game was over around eleven and we were heading home. As we left the soccer field riding our bikes, the sirens began sounding the alarm. The American bombers were coming through, as usual, heading northwest. We watched them with little concern. There were four groups of planes flying in formation, nine planes in each group, four-engine Liberators we thought. But this time instead of disappearing in the distance as in the past, they were turning around, hanging a one-eighty.

"Julius," I yelled, "Let's run! They are coming back! We're going to get hit!"

We were still in the middle of town, so there was no time to get out of the city. At the northern part of Szombathely, the bombs were already falling. On the southeast corner of St. Marton Road and King Street stood a hotel. It was the largest hotel in the city—maybe the only one—called the Palace.

The bombs were falling closer.

We could hear the explosions as they were coming closer and closer. The hotel was in front of us now. We knew that the hotel had a bomb shelter accessible from the street.

"Get down!" I yelled to Julius. We dropped our bicycles and ran for the shelter.

I opened the gate where they used to dump coal in peacetime and slid down the chute. Julius followed closely behind. It was pitch dark down there, but I sensed from the murmurs that there were quite a few people in the shelter.

Hotel guests, I thought first and for some reason having a lot of people around made me feel safer. When my eyes got used to the darkness I could see the people around me. There had to be around twenty of them, mostly women: maybe hotel employees, praying. The bombs were falling real close. The intensity of the prayer rose with each explosion. Then after a while the sound diminished, as did the intensity of the prayer, down to a trickle. Silence had arrived, but something was strange, a kind of precursor to something huge about to happen.

It did. Out of nowhere, came a strange whistling, whirling sound, growing louder by the second. It sounded like someone scratching a glass plate with a rusty nail.

My sixth sense told me that we were going to get hit. Hysteria broke out, men yelled at the top of their lungs, women screamed. The intensity of the sound increased to a cacophony. I was holding onto Julius's hand, dragging him with me under a bench. Then I lost his touch. The bomb hit the hotel with full impact.

It was Sunday noon.

By the time I crawled to the surface, one of a dozen people who came out alive—it was Sunday night. I could have dug myself out sooner, but I was determined to find Julius. I searched through rubble, crawled through caved-in walls; at times I was so buried with debris that I could no longer breathe. Sometimes my hands touched human bodies in dark cavities, probably dead bodies. Finally I surfaced, bruised, bleeding and despondent for not being able to find Julius. He was already home after digging himself out of the ruins earlier and searching for me. We met in Vep on Monday afternoon and swore friendship for life.

ONE HUNDRED THIRTY-SEVEN...
ONE HUNDRED THIRTY-EIGHT...

W E DID NOT LIKE JEWS. My mother could not forgive their biblical sin, not even nineteen centuries later. She knew every detail of the historical moment when the Jewish mob in Jerusalem, given a choice by Pontius Pilate as to which of the two criminals should go free, Jesus or Barabbas, their never to be forgiven sin was a unified scream: "Barabbas". To my mother that was the sin of all sins; she considered "them" responsible for the murder of the Son of God.

To her it was first-degree murder, no less.

My father had a more practical and timely reason for justifying disliking the Jews. On March 21, 1919, Bela Kun a Hungarian Jew rose to lead the Hungarian Bolshevik Revolution, which became legendary for their atrocities during what became known as the Red Terror. Hundreds of innocent Hungarians were brutally tortured and murdered by the Bolsheviks. Fashioned after Lenin's Dictatorship of the Proletariat in Russia, the dark memories of "The Chrysanthemum Revolution" that lasted for 133 days became permanently embedded in the mind of the average Hungarian. Since both Kun and his bloodthirsty henchman Tibor Szamuelly were Jewish, the anti-Semitic propaganda machine quickly churned the sentiment into national fervor. The majority of Hungarians, stunned by the brutality of the Red Terror, bought into the Jewish-Bolshevik conspiracy theory and the country arrived at a radically divided stage where you were either a Jew or you hated them.

My dad did not quite fit the pattern. He was not a Jew, and he may have disliked them for his own reason, but he harbored no hate in his heart either. He fought the Bolsheviks in 1919, volunteering to ride with the armored trains to defeat the forces of the Red Menace, Bela Kun. By the time the "White Terror" arrived to avenge its predecessor, my dad was already off the armored trains, having had a peacetime job with the railroad coupling freight trains and hoping to bring the economy of the land back to some acceptable level of peace and prosperity. Or at least it was so hoped.

Then the war came. Hitler, by 1944 after losing battle after battle, turned the remaining might of the Third Reich to complete his "historical mission", the extermination of the Jews of Europe.

The Hungarian railroad, the major transportation means of the country, was converted into endless caravans on steel wheels, rolling 400,000 Hungarian Jews to Auschwitz. The terror was led by the ever so anxious Arrow Cross gangs, determined to outdo their Nazi masters in brutality and savagery.

After capturing Budapest, the Soviet troops were marching west, virtually unopposed. Here and there the retreating Wermacht leftovers managed to mount small pockets of resistance to slow down the inevitable victory march of the Russians. Meanwhile the SS under Adolf

Eichmann, joined by the Hungarian Arrow Cross were putting together the "finishing touches" of Hitler's "ultimate mission." By mid-March 1945, most of the deportation to Auschwitz was completed and the trains were redirected to transport the last vestiges of the Reich escaping west just barely ahead of the Russians.

My dad worked at the Szombathely railroad station overseeing the status of freight railroad cars—what their content was, where they were heading, why they were stalled—helping to make some semblance of the chaos dominating the waning days of the war.

After finishing his shift he usually took the train from Szombathely to Vep; then walked home from the station either in the morning or early evening. Every other night he was home. It was sometime in mid-March, he was supposed to be coming home in the evening time as usual, but he did not. The evening got darker, and we, my mother and I, were beginning to get concerned. The train he should have taken was gone; he should have been home long ago. There were no bombing raids that day and we could not think of any reason why he was not home yet.

It must have been past midnight when I heard the street gate open, ever so gently, ever so slowly, as if someone opened it with the intention to muffle its creaking sound. I heard tiptoeing steps, soft murmuring sounds subdued conversation.

Walking through the front yard was my dad, with two shadowy figures beside him. One of them was tall, the other one short. They were all walking toward the tool shack; I heard its door open and close, then a bit later my father came into the house. He was a man of few words, but this night he was more quiet than usual. I was already in bed and could hear faint conversation, an exchange of short sentences, but could not make out what they were talking about. All I noticed was that my mother's voice sounded full of apprehension and concern. Then dad left the kitchen and went to the tool shack again where he stayed for what seemed to be an unreasonably long time. Eventually my mother came into our small bedroom—all three of us slept in that small room in two separate beds—and she softly spoke to me.

"Your dad brought two Jews. He does not want to talk about it now. Maybe tomorrow he will. Maybe he won't. God help us!"

My dad came back to the bedroom a short while later; he went to sleep without saying a word.

***

Due to the bombing raids, the schools had already been closed for months. Dad had his day off, so mother prepared breakfast: goat milk, a slice of smoked bacon with bread and onion. The front was less than a hundred kilometers east, moving fast. People figured that the Russians would get to the village in a few days, maybe a week, for sure no more than two. The search for Jews diminished. Only some anxious wannabe Arrow Cross thugs, now on their own without the SS or the Gestapo, were determined to find Jews in hiding.

"I want you to stay away from the tool shack!" my dad turned and spoke to me between two bites of bread. We finished the breakfast in silence; then the story unfolded.

***

"I was checking a bunch of freight cars for cargo," my father began his story." They were parked in the backyard of the station, moved there late afternoon. Most cars were full of bales of dry hay some others had construction materials, mostly cement bags stacked end to end. When I got to one boxcar, the gate was already open. I rolled the side door wide, inside were four cows tied to the inside wall. They were making a lot of noise. I thought that they had not been fed for some time. I was thinking about bringing some hay from the other wagon when something caught my attention. A shadow seemed to be moving in the corner behind the cows. Hesitantly I stepped inside of the boxcar and took a second look."

"Please don't hurt us," said a voice from the dark corner of the car, "please don't!"

"I bring you no harm," I said to a shadow emerging from the dark corner. It was a tall, fragile phantom-like creature, slowly moving toward me. I was somewhat concerned because I noticed that another shadow was still lurking in the corner, who knows with what intention or maybe even with weapons.

The fragile shadow, as if reading my thoughts, spoke to me: "That's my son, Josef. He is ten and he means no harm. We are Jews and we are very hungry. We have not eaten for two days."

When I told him that I would bring them some food from the station for I had some leftover from lunch, he got extremely agitated:

"Please don't bring the police or the Arrow Cross. They will kill us. Please!"

I gave him my word that it would be only food, although not a lot. There was a bit of pork sausage left with a large chunk of bread. I filled up a jug with tap water and headed back for the freight car where I found them.

They were no longer there.

I had a strong suspicion that they did not trust me, and understood them. Whatever they had gone through—which I was yet to learn—they had every reason not to trust anyone. So I decided to stay around and about ten minutes later came to realize that I guessed right. They were hiding six cars away probably watching me, waiting. Not that it would do any good for them to hide had I brought the Arrow Cross or even just the railroad security; they would be killed just the same. Now they were tiptoeing back toward me, turning their heads from side to side like frightened animals. It was beginning to get dark so I moved all of us into a freight car that was relatively empty and handed the food over to them. The scene was a heartbreaker, they were not eating: they were devouring food without even taking a breath in between.

Their story was a tearful one.

His name was Ignac; his son was ten with a non- traditional Jewish like name, Josef. In the nineteen thirties, some Jewish families sensing the winds of the coming Nazi persecution gave their children non-Jewish sounding names.

They were from Sopron, the westernmost city in Hungary, right at the Austrian border. His wife was rounded up weeks earlier. The Arrow Cross missed Ignac and his son until just a couple of days ago. As they were herding them along with dozen of others into boxcars somehow they managed to escape from the train headed for Auschwitz, probably the last one. They found a hiding place in a parked train. They had no idea where the train was going, all they knew that it was not the "death train". It did not move until the next morning; then it started to roll but they still had no idea where to. He and his son settled into an empty corner. The train stopped for hours, later moved on again. They fell asleep, slept throughout the rest of next night and part of another day until I ran into them," said my dad as he finished the saga of Ignac and his son Josef.

Now what?

They did not ask my father to take them to our home: they knew the potential consequences. But they did not have to; my father had more compassion in his heart than Hitler had armies left. He already had made a decision to hide them at our home. The Russians were just weeks, maybe days away: the Germans were preoccupied with the retreat. The real danger was the Hungarian countryside gendarme and the Arrow Cross.

The hardest part of the mission was to get them both to our home.

They could not take the train from Szombathely to Vep, for obvious reasons they had to walk. The distance was about seven kilometers between the two. The road, a poorly maintained country road was usually deserted, especially at night, but not in these days. Caravans of German trucks, loaded with the exhausted troops of the once mighty

Third Reich, were headed home or whatever was left of their home in Germany. They were the last people you wanted to run into with two Jews by your side.

So they took the back roads, rarely traveled trails between cornfields. It took over five hours to get to our house.

And now they were hiding in the cellar of the tool shack. Actually it was a relatively safe hiding place. A few years back, Dad and I dug a cellar into the ground under the floor of the shack. The cellar was just a big square hole in the ground, about five feet long by five feet wide and about five feet deep. It was supposed to be a cold place to store pork food items throughout the hot summer days. The floor of the shack was fashioned into a trap door level with the floor of the shack and once it was lowered, it made the cellar a perfect albeit tight hiding place for two people from the eyes of a casual searcher. The shack had a small window from where one could see the street gate. And, of course, there was Rajna, our German shepherd, nobody passed by her without her serious and loud objection. It was March, the weather was cold; our pork sausage and bacon were still in the smoke shack.

"They will stay there during the day. One of them will watch the street gate at all times during daylight. If the gate opens and Rajna barks, they are to head into the cellar with the trapdoor closed. At night, they will sleep in the shack, my father said. "And I don't want either of you going near the tool shack until I tell you so!"

"Can I meet them?" I asked my father.

"No you can't!"

My mother was freaking out: "Do you have any idea what the Arrow Cross…" My dad did not let her finish:

"You need not to tell me. You two know nothing about them hiding there. It's all me."

"They will kill you," my mother cried out.

"Too late to worry about that. If we report them, their blood will be on our hands forever."

"But they killed the Son of God," came my mother's last argument.

My dad had enough. I knew when he drew the proverbial line in the sand, seldom as he did, but when he did it was as solid as the Great Wall of China.

Apparently, this was one of those times.

"I don't have to go back to work for a few days, maybe the Russians will get here; they are close. In the meantime, the Jews will stay. I will bring them food and water; they will not get out of the shack. You both stay away."

And that was the end of the conversation. The Russians did not arrive in Vep for another eight days or so, but the Arrow Cross people were seen less and less in the village. Their local head left a few days before the first Soviet troops arrived. Ignac and his son mysteriously disappeared Thursday night, just a day before the arrival of the Russians.

***

My father had a Doxa pocket watch that he believed was lost while climbing in and out of the boxcars. He was saddened the watch was one of his precious possessions. He asked Ignac whether he remembered seeing it, but he said he did not.

We never learned what happened to Ignac and his son. About five years later, my dad still worked for the railroad, now at the Vep station standing by the train as it stopped usually for a short time. One day, a young stranger stepped off the train, walked right up to my dad and addressed him by his name. My father answered:

"Yah, that's me!"

"I've got a present for you then," said the stranger and placed a small box into my dad's hand. Before dad could take a second look, the stranger was back on the train and gone.

My dad opened the carefully packaged box.

There was a Doxa pocket watch with two dates engraved into the cover: the date of their arrival and the date of their departure from the cellar of our tool shack. The initials were "I" and "J".

Oh yes, it was a brand new Doxa, the cover and the heavy chain were pure gold. Easily was worth more than a few months' salary of my dad.

ONE HUNDRED SIXTY-ONE...
ONE HUNDRED SIXTY-TWO...

THE FRONT WAS RAPIDLY MOVING WEST. By the end of March we could hear artillery from the distance, sounding like muffled thunder. On Wednesday, March 28, a German truck rode up the hill where we lived and stopped in front of several homes, including ours. A couple of German soldiers came through the gate. My mother stood in their way, but only for a moment. They shoved her aside and grabbed me by the arm.

"Let's go!"

"Where are you taking my son?" she cried.

"Just to dig some foxholes," answered one of the Germans in fluent Hungarian. "He'll be back in the morning!" The truck took me along with a bunch of other kids some from Vep, others from neighboring villages. We were driven all the way to a wide river called Raba, about 20 miles east.

There the front was really close maybe 20 to 30 miles. The Russians were coming on the eastern shore of the river, the Germans on the western shore, preparing to take a stand. We were digging foxholes about 300 yards from the river. Behind us was a cemetery, surrounded by high brick walls. In the center on the top of the hill, was a chapel. I could see a German machine gun sticking through the opening of the chapel wall facing east, directly above our heads.

Somewhere in the distance, farther west beyond the cemetery, was the old Hungarian city, Sarvar. We were digging foxholes all Wednesday afternoon. The Germans were passing out Mannlicher rifles and sacks of ammunition along with bean soup in aluminum pots and day-old dark bread. Then we dug more holes and connecting trenches.

Later in the night light snow fell. By Thursday morning we were all shivering and shaking, whether from the cold or from fear, I could not tell. Along with the dawn came the first Russian, part of a landing group. He was wearing a "pufajka", a kind of a heavy quilted jacket, with his "guitar", a submachine gun, tossed across his shoulder. A few dozen kids with WWI rifles ready to stop the Soviet war machine! Covered with freshly fallen snow, with their hands shaking, their fingers on cold steel triggers, watching his every move.

The machine gun in the chapel began to fire, sounding like popcorn crackling.

Then we ran; out of the foxholes between the graves, out of the cemetery.

The Russian artillery must have been called in because they were now heavily bombarding the west bank of the river. Half the cemetery was taken out, including the chapel on the hill with the German machine gun.

No more weddings here, baby, I thought as I ran.

In the meantime, all hell broke loose at the riverbank. The artillery fire kept changing targets; most of us were out of range with the bombardment behind us. I decided to run until I could hitch onto some westbound retreating German vehicle.

The war had its surprises.

By the time I got to Sarvar the battle was already raging on the city streets. Eventually I ended up at the south side of the city where the fighting was on, door to door. One street corner was occupied with Russians, the next one with Germans. About three blocks away, I spotted my salvation: a German armored truck moving in a stop and go fashion westward. In order to reach it, there were two city blocks to pass through first, occupied mostly with Russians. The movement of the troops had no pattern to it. After a few seconds the two corners were clear of soldiers, except one tall Russian with his back to me. He was peeking out from behind the corner down on to the next street, his back a perfect target for me. I never had or intended to kill anyone, but it seemed that might soon change!

I had to get to that German truck to get home to safety before it moved out of my reach.

To safety? With the Germans ahead and the Russians behind?

Regardless, home was still a home, I had to get there and this Russian was in my way. Slowly, I raised the gun; my hand was shaking. I thought it was the weight of the gun. Or maybe it was the weight of the killing I was going to commit, the weight which had already started to burden my soul. The gun kept getting heavier as I was raising it. The Russian's back was a welcoming invite to the small targeting access on the long barrel of the gun.

Lots of thoughts were swirling in my head while I was making the final, almost unconscious decision to kill a man. *Who was he? Was he married? Had he left a kid home somewhere in some forlorn Khazak village, maybe a kid just like me, who was waiting for him to come home one day from the war? Waiting and waiting and for how long? When was he going to accept the fact that his father would never again come home to see him?*

Would he ever know that a young, 14-year-old Hungarian boy, maybe just like him, in some strange, never-before-heard-of city, somewhere thousands of miles away, would end his father's return forever by moving his index finger another quarter of an inch?

All the shooting and killing around me, including my own carefully aimed rifle and the impending fatal shot, created strange images and memories. It felt like being in the carnival that used to come to Vep every second Sunday once a year in August. There was one tent I liked a lot, for a coin I could shoot at metal ducks traveling on wire tracks with white circles painted on their side. When I hit the white spot with a bullet from a BB gun, the duck fell over and the carnival man gave me a stuffed giraffe. Somehow this felt much the same.

Except here there were no ducks, just soldiers, and they did not have white spots painted on their sides. If you missed, they shot back. And nobody gave away stuffed giraffes.

Let's do it; I have to get home. My finger got instruction from my brain, processing the order to pull the trigger. It could not have been more than a nanosecond when suddenly the Russian started to fall forward. At first it appeared that he made a move to run, but he just kept on falling until he was flat on the pavement. Then I realized that a second earlier before he started falling, I had heard the sound of a single gunshot. And it dawned on me that it was not my gun, my right index finger was still a blink away from moving the trigger. The Russian was now on the pavement spread out at a weird angle still in a position as if running, now in two dimensions. A small puddle of blood around his head, a dark red crown was growing slowly.

I dropped the gun and ran for the German truck. Two German soldiers reached down as I got next to the side of the truck and pulled me on board. For them the war was just about over, they were heading west. The retreating German front was collapsing. I got home Thursday evening to find that our little house was full of strangers.

As the front rolled west, more and more Hungarians were moving along, just ahead of the Russian troops, hoping to reach American-occupied territories before the Russians caught up with them. Nobody knew how far east the American troops would get. But when these west-moving Hungarians got close to the border of Austria and were ready to leave their homeland, maybe forever, many of them changed their minds and decided to stop running and to stay in Hungary.

That's how in the small home where I lived with my parents, a dozen relatives ended up, half of them women.

ONE HUNDRED EIGHTY-FIVE...
ONE HUNDRED EIGHTY-SIX...

The main Russian troops got to the village late Friday, March 30th. The battles ceased; there was no more fighting. The villagers knew that raping, pillaging and senseless destruction by drunken Russian troops were part of the war. People were prepared for the worst. Since brutal raping was the most feared, women of all ages went into hiding.

The oldest woman in our home was my grandmother. The youngest was my cousin, Marci, around sixteen. Men folk staying at our house decided that all women should go into hiding. We had a small kitchen with a narrow door leading into an even smaller narrow pantry. The plan was to move the women into the pantry, shut the door and put a large credenza in front of the door to cover it up completely. Since the pantry was very narrow, no one would ever suspect any hiding space behind the credenza, we hoped.

Shortly before the Russians arrived, the women were already huddling in the pantry.

The first Russian contingent came through about seven in the evening. They were too drunk to notice the strangeness of seven men and no women. Besides, all they wanted was booze, and when they found none, they kicked doors and the dog on their way out.

As it was a lull in the "visiting" of troops, some of the men in the house, including my dad, thought that having seven men and no women looked too suspicious, so maybe we should put three or four men into the pantry and bring out our grandma. She was definitely too old to be a rape subject. And maybe another older woman, masked with soot to look old and ugly. There was some debate as to which men should go into hiding and which men should stay in the kitchen. Finally a decision was reached. We had just started to move the credenza when the next Russian group moved through the street gate. There was only a moment's time to shove the credenza back to cover the pantry door. The kitchen was still full of men and no women.

The Russians were led by a short, stocky Mongol-looking major, evil in his eyes set far apart like his cheekbones.

They were angry and drunk. The major kept pushing the men around with the butt of his submachine gun; he was livid. He was rummaging through the rest of the house, knocking over furniture, breaking dishes.

He sensed that there was something odd here.

He was walking up and down in the kitchen, to the bedroom, then back to the kitchen. Apparently it seemed obvious to him that if there were seven men, six of them grown-ups, there had to be women around. With obvious reluctance, finally they were about to leave. The major was the last one to move out. As he stepped into the doorway, he changed his mind. He turned around, made a step back into the kitchen, swung his "guitar" around his shoulder, and aimed it at the glass door of the credenza with stacks of porcelain dishes behind the glass.

Then he pulled the trigger, spraying bullets.

One of the women in the pantry panicked and started screaming. The remaining five Russians were on their way out now turned around and came back. They dragged the credenza away, found the door, found the women. They were herded into the kitchen, lined them up against the wall. The men, including me, lined up against the opposite wall of the kitchen separated by six proud Russian heroes. Five of them were pointing their "guitars" at seven shaking men. The sixth, the major with the wide set evil eyes, was checking out the "merchandise".

When he got to my cousin, Ilu, who was twenty years old, and the third one in the line-up, he stopped.

"No, no, no!" yelled her fiancé as he fell to the feet of the brute, begging.

One of the other soldiers swung his submachine gun around and brought the butt down on his head until there was silence. The major grabbed Ilu's arm, dragged her to the center of the kitchen, swung his weapon off his shoulder and handed it to one of the other soldiers. Then with both hands, he reached for the clothes around her shoulders and ripped them all the way down to the floor. Once he was through, the remaining five followed. She was raped by all of them, handing their submachine guns to the next in line, unbuttoning, dropping their pants halfway; performing the ultimate act of heroism!

I could swear that by the time the sixth brave Soviet hero was raping her that she was unconscious, maybe dead.

My father fell to his knees.

"God, oh God! Where are you?"

My dad was an extremely religious man and he never questioned His whereabouts before. But God certainly had to be away that day. Maybe because it was Good Friday 1945 and his Beloved Son Jesus had been nailed to the cross on the hills of Golgotha almost two millennia ago.

ONE HUNDRED NINETY...
ONE HUNDRED NINETY-ONE...

COMMUNISM BECAME THE WORD OF CHANGE, THE WORD OF HOPE. Oppressors, oligarchs, barons and baronesses, princes and princesses, feudal landlords, go away! We've had enough of you! Nobody wanted any more of them!

Yes, it was possible that there were answers better than what the Communists offered, but if there were, nobody seemed to propose them. Both of my parents were deeply religious people; to them Communism was the "evil of all evils". Back in 1943 when we moved back to Vep, they enrolled me into a parochial high school, run by a French religious teaching order of the Premontre Saint Norbert in Szombathely. My education had cost my father at least half of his salary until I got a scholarship a year later. My parents hoped that someday I would become a "Messenger of God", a Catholic priest. By the time I graduated at age eighteen, I spoke three languages including Latin, was able to solve differential equations and quote English classics by heart.

Thanks to the teaching of the Premontre monks.

The end of the war for Hungary was April 4, 1945. The Communists were already on the move. In that year they received less than 20 percent of the popular vote, yet they managed to secure key government positions, the drive was on to control the country. Beginning in late 1948, by "popular demand", they took over the schools, including the one I attended. The priests were quickly disposed of; some were sent to prison, others just disappeared. A few managed to escape across the border to Austria. The Iron Curtain was in the process of being built. The priests were replaced by government appointed civilian teachers and the discipline, as well as the quality of education, dropped drastically. Fortunately for me and my education, it was my last year in the school.

Julius went to a different school, but most of us kids rode the same train from Vep to Szombathely in the morning and back to the village in the evening. I still considered him a friend, but it seemed that our relationship had cooled off. Maybe it was because Julius and his family were atheists and my parents were religious people. They called us bigots.

There were a lot of fights on the train, I tried to stay away from them. I came to a conclusion that I was not born to be a fighter. Violence never seemed to offer a solution to anything. I became nervous with butterflies in my stomach at any confrontation.

One day on the train an argument broke out between Julius and Steve Boka. When I stepped in between them, trying to stop the coming fight, Julius hit me straight in the face. Deliberately. At first, I could not believe it. It was not that it hurt me, although my nose started bleeding. Julius was bigger and stronger than me. I considered fighting back then decided against it.

"You should not have done that, Julius," I said, as I was wiping off the blood.

The kids had no mercy.

"Zak the Chicken! Zak the Chicken!"

The next day I went to a boxing gym in Szombathely and took up boxing. Also I found that one of the boxing instructors was a sensei in Kung Fu. I began to take karate lessons.

Life moved on with high hopes.

The church in one of the villages near Vep was damaged during the last days of the war and had to be rebuilt. The Communist Party led the reconstruction efforts. The church was rebuilt; the Communists took credit. When the huge estates of the landlords were to be redistributed amongst the landless, fulfilling a thousand-year-old dream of the toilers of the land, it was the Communist Party carrying the chain measuring out the land to its new owners.

A new social order was on its unstoppable way.

The devastating postwar inflation ended, and while the Communists had nothing to do with stabilizing the currency, they managed to take credit for it. Young people like me, for whom the only athletic activity until the Communists came to power was working in the fields for the landlords, now could join youth organizations. There I could play tennis on courts previously reserved for the privileged, we could drive motorcycles, play soccer, learn boxing, gymnastics, skydiving, the world! New universities were built, no longer for the children of the aristocracy.

The Communists were the movers, powering the change.

Some disturbing signs began to appear on the horizon. During 1948 and 1949, one industrial complex after another was hit by arson, some burned to the ground. Somehow the Communist Party was always able to find the "arsonist," who admitted that he was hired by the capitalist owners of the factory to burn the plant to the ground "rather than let the new order take it over." It took years to learn that the wholesale arson was a ploy engineered by the Communists, designed to create a public outcry, a "popular demand" to justify the nationalization of Hungary's entire industrial complex.

Then the Iron Curtain was built.

The project was supposed to be a secret, but how could something 60 feet wide, over a hundred miles long that required hundreds of workers to build remain secret?! Then priests here and there were kidnapped in the dead of night by "thugs" - thugs who never got caught. The priests disappeared, churches closed down.

Then the youth clubs profile began to change. If you were not a member of the Communist Youth League, you had less and less access to the activities of the clubs.

In the political arena, the Communists were the only ones with strategy and organizational structure.

In June 1948, the Communists made a bold move and joined the Social Democrats in a coalition, acquiring majority. On the first of February, 1949, an innocent-sounding coalition by the name of The Independent People's Front was created, which then was converted into the Hungarian Workers Party. On May 15, 1949, the election was won by the Hungarian Workers Party (96.2%). A Stalin-like dictatorship under Matyas Rakosi, Stalin's henchman, was then installed.

The Small Landholders Party and the Social Democrats, since they were no longer needed, were ruthlessly crushed into oblivion by the Communist power structure. Within less than three years, all the land distributed with the help of the Communist Party earlier was forced into the state-owned farmers co-operatives, the "kolhoz." Four million Hungarians now toiled the land for a new and evermore oppressive landlord, the Communist state.

The Iron Curtain was completed and declared to be foolproof. Some churches, including the ones rebuilt with Communist help just a few years back, were now closed, some were designated as government warehouses.

Cardinal Mindszenty, the last flickering hope of religious freedom in Hungary and a lonely voice in the wilderness, was arrested, tried for treason, and sentenced to death. His sentence was later commuted to life imprisonment.

ONE HUNDRED NINETY-EIGHT...
ONE HUNDRED NINETY-NINE...

M Y FIRST LOVE—OR AT LEAST SO I THOUGHT—WAS A GIRL IN
SZOMBATHELY BY THE NAME OF MARIKA. I was seventeen when
I met her through her brother Otto who was my schoolmate.
She and I took our relationship seriously.

Her family was typical of a Hungarian middle class before the
war. Her father—of German descent—was conductor in a pre-
Communist Hungarian Army, a baton wielder in front of a military
marching band. He was a short guy, who considered life a serious
proposition, an old timer who believed in honor and integrity. When
the Communists disbanded the Hungarian military forces to be
replaced by the People's Army, Marika's father lost his lifetime job.
He eventually got employed as a laborer in a textile factory where he
was told to volunteer on socialist holidays for the same baton wielding

for the factory's marching band. *("We the children of Stalin, we march together for a socialist world of peace,"* etc. etc.*)*

"Nobody is unemployed in the socialist society" was the Party's edict and Uncle Paul (that was his first name) was marching faithfully in front of an equally un-cheerful volunteer marching brigade in the process of building socialism.

Otto, the brother of my love was a bright kid, arrogant and cocky but it fit me just fine. Even though I became almost a family member, probably spending more time at their home than at mine, I never felt fully accepted. I felt more tolerated than liked. Probably I was too much of an individual for the family's taste. It was in the second year of our relationship when Marika and her father got an invitation to a wedding from their relatives who lived in a village about 50 miles northwest of Szombathely.

The year was 1948, the beginning of my last year in the eight year gymnasium. The year was a turbulent one. Our high school was run by the Brothers of the Premontre St. Norbert Teaching Order. The Communists were already acquiring power positions in the government and targeted education as key to sustained power. They simply needed to get rid of the brothers and replace them with their own ideologists. The project was already in trouble; people were uneasy about moving too fast: children were still "taboo". The Communists needed more justification for their actions.

That was the political landscape of the days. The invitation of Uncle Paul and Marika's was more than being wedding guests; she was to be a bridesmaid. I was not invited and to me it was an insult.

I've got to be there, I decided. The task was not easy, but when was the last time that difficulty deterred me?

The village, called Kereszteny was a relatively small township, maybe 2000 residents. It had a small railroad station, more like a large guardhouse, where the trains, two maybe three during a given day, stopped briefly or just rolled through. It was September 1948 I was seventeen years old and full of romance. Innocent and ignorant. What I did not know was that Kereszteny was right at the Austrian-Hungarian border just a couple of miles away, and the building of the Iron Curtain was already in progress.

Lack of knowledge can be a terrible handicap!

I started to make plans for my uninvited visit. As the days went by, my jealousy was getting the best of me. A powerful, and at times deadly, emotion as I had the chance to learn about it. My first encounter with it had all the raw edges.

I needed an accomplice, a "partner" to get things done. I recruited one of my buddies, Matthew. He was a free spirit with an enterprising soul. When I shared my plan with him all he could say was that the idea was totally crazy. I told him that he had to tell me something else, I already knew that. So he did:

"Crazy, but it sounds fun!" he said.

To be around the wedding and observe Marika's behavior without her knowing it, I needed a disguise. The disguise I came up with I thought was simply brilliant.

To be disguised as a chimneysweeper.

Chimneysweepers usually went about their job in pairs. One of them was the sweeper, actually doing the job of cleaning the chimneys. He was outfitted with all the imaginable gear that the performance of his profession called for, including a black fez-like cap, a bandana around the forehead extending into a black wraparound of the ears down to the neck. The rest of the outfit was even better, at least for my purpose. A black tight jacket buttoned up all the way to the neck, with a tall collar that was blended into the wraparound coming from the headgear. It came up so high that most of the time it covered the chin terminating at the lower lip. The pants were to match: black long pants with high boots laced all the way to the knees to end up the outfit with knee-patches. To be sure that the face was fully protected—in my case disguised—chimneysweepers usually wore large dark goggles.

The gear was not any less spectacular. A ten foot long wire ending up in a metal brush, where the wire was wrapped into a neat circular shape fitting perfectly around one's shoulder on one side, while on the other shoulder was a similar gadget but instead of a wire brush it was a 3 pound metal ball designed to knock off resisting petrified patches of soot.

After creating a semi-convincing lie and a small bribe, I borrowed a full outfit, except the complex gear, from a local legitimate chimneysweeper, his reserve uniform for my thrilling adventure. Matthew needed no special uniform. A team of operating chimneysweepers consisted of the one who swept and the other who supervised and was not in uniform. Marika or her father had never seen Matthew, so for him no disguise was necessary.

The train left Szombathely before dawn; we were traveling in separate cars. The real test came getting off the train in Kereszteny. Only four people got off, Marika, her father, Matthew and me. A half a dozen or so relatives were at the small station, waiting. As we were getting off the train a cheer went up singing the folklore:

"I saw a chimneysweeper,
These newlyweds will be lucky"

***

We passed the first test with flying colors. Maybe "flying black" would've been a better term. The walk from the station was not too long except for the boots that I got along with the borrowed outfit. They were at least two sizes too large. It took us some time, but time we had plenty of. The real wedding celebration was not scheduled until later on in the afternoon. Before noon, the church ceremonies were conducted, but they were of no interest to me; not a place for sinning. The big event, the party with drinking and dancing was to take place at the house, lasting possibly into the night.

Matthew said he was going to take the earliest train back to Szombathely, no matter what. He seemed to be somewhat uneasy now about the whole thing and then he made what turned out to be a deadly mistake. Rather than carrying the backpack with my regular clothing, he asked the stationmaster if he could leave the backpack in the small cubbyhole at the station. The stationmaster agreed. As I later on reflected, he agreed just a bit too readily, but I was too preoccupied to listen to my sixth sense.

The village was maybe a dozen streets; one looked like the main street, with a few shorter ones branching off. The house where the wedding was to be held looked rather obvious. The fence was decorated with balloons, flurry of activities, lots of people walking in and out. The house looked like one of the largest in the village amongst a few hundred homes. It had a large backyard, twice the size of the neighbors'. A huge storage barn was separating the inner yard from a large field behind which could have been a couple of acres of what looked like cornfields.

A large walnut tree, just as if made for the "mission", towered behind the barn. It was considerably taller than the top of the barn, providing an ideal lookout for viewing the activities of the inner yard where the party was going to happen. Being September, the tree was richly clothed with leaves provided great cover.

To kill time, Matthew and I made a few house calls. While I was not about to engage in knocking and sweeping soot off the chimneys, we made what looked like professional observations. Matthew took copious notes and set up appointments to come back next week, we concocted false stories as to why the regular guys did not show, and assured people that we were just doing inspections, their regular chimneysweeper would be back as usual.

Time came to approach the walnut tree.

The climbing was easier than I thought. In spite of my armor-like outfit I climbed the tree with ease. I was a gymnast in school; not the best but this was no difficult task either. I sat on the tree watching the party where absolutely nothing of any consequence that could be of interest to me was happening. Marika looked sweet, but there were none of my fantasies of her hugging, kissing a stranger, or God knows what else. She acted as if bored by the whole event, as if she did not belong, and could hardly wait to get the whole thing over with. I was immensely embarrassed.

What's wrong with me? Where did my sick jealousy come from? What's the unwarranted suspicion for? Don't I look like a total idiot sitting on a walnut tree, in a chimneysweeper outfit?

The sun still was high above the horizon when I climbed down from the tree and started out to the railroad station. Matthew got tired of the whole scene a lot earlier and headed back to the station to catch a train back to Szombathely. Maybe he was already gone. I could hardly wait to get to the station and change back into my street clothing, fold the silly uniform into the backpack, get out of there and try to forget the whole idiotic adventure. Fate however had a different plan in mind. As I approached the station, I got suspicious but I could not quite figure out what brought on the uneasiness. Then I spotted two bicycles propped up against the station's wall. I looked around, did not see anyone, and tried to settle my mind.

Two bicycles, so what, I told myself and walked into the station.

Matthew was sitting on a wooden bench. In front of him the backpack, with my clothing spread across the floor. Two uniformed cops were standing around, local police officers, apparently the owners of the bikes. For a fleeting moment I thought to run, for another moment I was going to yell to Matthew don't tell anything, but then I realized that it was too late for either. Nowhere to run and probably Matthew had already spilled the beans.

He sure did.

There was no way to come up with a substitute version; Matthew already gave enough details making his story non-retractable. Any attempt at a denial was useless. One of the two cops, the younger one, the more stupid looking of the two, although higher in rank, kept repeating.

"This happens only in the movies, in those American movies. Only in the movies."

Finally after some discussion, they decided to get proof of Matthew's story: "Let's go to the wedding, maybe they'll invite us for a drink!" and with that the party was ready to depart. Two cops with their bikes and me in between them. To be identified whether I am really who Matthew said I am. It took me seventeen troubled years and a fool-hearted short trip to a small never before heard of Hungarian village to learn for the rest of my life what humiliation and embarrassments are really like.

First I refused to go. So they twisted my arms behind me and I was safely and surely handcuffed. Then I asked to change my clothing, not a chance. Reluctantly, I walked with them back to the wedding place into the midst of the happy celebration. I have no way—not even now six decades later—to describe my shame and humiliation as I stood against the wall handcuffed, decked out in a chimneysweeper outfit. When the music stopped, the dancing came to an abrupt end the cops asked if anybody knew me. Uncle Paul walked up to me. He lifted my dark glasses gazed into my face and with a look of sad disappointment, he murmured.

"Yeah, we know him!"

Then I was let go. My head bowed in shame. As I walked out of the house, the last thing I heard was the younger cop saying: "Would you believe, just like in the movies."

I never found out whether they were invited for a drink or not.

***

I was on my way back to the station, I still needed to reclaim my street clothes. Most likely, the train with Matthew was already gone to Szombathely, but hopefully the station master—probably he was the one who called the cops after searching the backpack Matthew had left with him—was still around so that I could get my precious clothing.

A Jeep passed me by; I paid no attention, I was deep in my soul-tearing thoughts. When I looked up I saw that about fifty yards ahead of me, it had stopped. As I got closer I recognized the occupants: AVO agents. Strangely though, their shoulder pad was not blue as the AVO's, but green. Oh, I thought, the border patrol version of the dreaded AVO, called AVH. What were they doing here? Then it hit me: I must be close to the Austrian Hungarian border and I remembered hearing rumors that they were building some barbed wire border fence, not allowing any more traffic across the border.

"Where you going comrade?" came the inevitable greetings as I got close.

There was not a lot that I could say, but I was determined not to tell the truth, no matter what. Rather die than go through the same humiliation again. The one in the passenger seat got out of the Jeep, blocking my way. There was no need for that; I was not going anywhere. No more visit to the wedding house, no more Uncle Paul, no more "Yes, we know him". Let them just assume that I was trying to cross their precious border, if that's what it was all about.

Apparently, it was.

The border—became known as the Iron Curtain—was under construction less than a few miles away, unbeknownst to me. These two were scratching their head trying to figure out what to do with me. I was probably their first catch. Then they told me to get into the back seat. The AVH guy, who was on the passenger side of the Jeep, leaned back into the car and got on what looked like a shortwave radio an elaborate gadget in the center. After dialing he had a conversation going. I did not like the way he talked, looking at me, nodding his head, the facial expressions were signaling troubles. I assumed by looking at his face that some new interest was developing.

"Hold" he said to someone on the other end. He then turned to me.

"What's your name?"

I told him.

"Are you a student?"

I saw no reason to deny that either.

"What school you going to?"

I realized that I was on the short end of the proverbial stick, nowhere to go. So I told him.

He went back to his short wave conversation for quite some time. Then he turned to me again:

"Are you on the Dozsa boxing team?"

"*Geez,*" I was wondering what my short popularity as a boxer would yield me. I tried to be funny.

"You want my autograph?"

His mental portfolio had not contained any appreciation for lighthearted comments. He took my smart-ass remark as a "yes" for his question regarding my boxing team then returned to his radio, had a few "affirmatives", then turned to the driver who seemed to have no interest in the ongoing conversation until now when his buddy said:

"We are takin' him in!"

"In where?" asked the driver.

I actually had the same question in mind, without asking it though, soon I would know.

"To King Street."

"Hey," the driver lightened up "Szombathely, eh?"

"*Patrolling the borders must have been a hell of a boring job*" I came to the conclusion noticing the obvious excitement the announcement caused.

"Have you got any decent clothes?" asked the AVH guy, just off the phone.

"At the station."

"Great, let's roll," said the driver sticking the shift into gear and the Jeep was on its way with two excited AVH soldiers and one seventeen year old boy scared out of his wits.

First, we drove by the railroad station to pick up my stuff. Matthew was gone; the clothes were back in the back-pack. I looked at the stationmaster from a distance. I saw an evil smile on his face as he talked to the AVH man who was picking up my backpack. I knew for sure now what his role was, the informer the essential cog in the wheel called tyranny.

The AVO building in Szombathely had a dark reputation. People, if they had to walk on King Street, went on to the other side of the street long before they got close to the building. It was a gray three-story high, ugly looking building, dominating the end corner of one of Szombathely's two main boulevards. After about an hour drive we arrived in a small alley separating a closed-up movie-theater from the AVO head quarter's south side, a forbidden street for pedestrians. If the building looked ominous on the outside, it was nothing when compared to what it looked on the inside. As soon as we drove across the sidewalk, the Jeep had to make a 90 degree turn to the right in order to enter through an electronically controlled gate which buzzed with a half dozen short but deafening screams. It was pitch dark at first until the driver turned on the headlights and slowed to almost a full stop to navigate the sharp turn. We arrived to another gate this one was controlled by an armed AVO man.

The AVH guy from the passenger side got up, talked to the guard, pointed a couple times toward me, then proceeded to sign some papers and came back to the car. Opening the door on the passenger's side, he told me to get out.

"You'll be processed. Hope you had a joyful ride!" His voice was full of sarcasm. Processing meant giving a whole bunch of information to one of two guards, meanwhile I saw from the corner of my eyes that the Jeep slowly maneuvered out of the area severing my last connection with the outside world. Then I heard the buzzer again and the snapping of the gate a bit later.

"We don't need chimney sweeping here Miska, do we?" the larger of the two AVO said to the other guy. The shorter one looked real spooky to me. There was something about him, but I had no idea what it was, until later. I had to change into my street clothes. The chimney sweeper uniform was not an easy garb to remove, but piece by piece they were coming off. I got to my underwear and was reaching for my regular pants when the weirdo looking guard, called Miska, stopped me.

"What about your shorts, boy?" he said with a look on his face that scared me.

"I'll keep those on," I said meekly.

"Oh no, you don't! Not 'til I say you do. Let me just look at you close pretty boy!"

By now I had a good guess where he was heading, but had no idea what to do about it. I was more scared than confused.

"Take it off boy, I said take it off!"

I did not move. I was petrified. He then made a step toward me, I started backing off but did not get far because the wall behind my back stopped me. He was close breathing heavily his breath was like an onion gas pump, blowing right into my face. I screamed.

The taller guard, who so far showed only a slightly annoyed face, now spoke up.

"Leave the kid alone, Miska."

Apparently his voice did not sound convincing enough, Miska was not about to stop. Then suddenly out of nowhere came the irritating sound of a buzzer again. *Oh, what a relief!* This time it sounded like chiming church bells at the end of the holy mass, celebrating. Miska rose to his feet, the entire scene changed reminding me of a theatrical rehearsal stage.

"Get the gate," said the taller guard. Miska reluctantly shrugged his shoulder and left. The other guard stood around while I put my pants and shirt on. "I'll take you in," he said "before Miska comes back. He is weird sometimes, can't help it. Weird, yeah, real weird. I don't know if they will keep him."

The cell he led me to was a couple of levels lower judged by counting the stairs as I followed him down a narrow walkway with a dangling light-bulb here and there. More than a dozen steps later we arrived at an enlarged area with three doors opening into an odd shaped landing. The guard took out a bunch of keys on a large metal ring, tried a few, until finally one worked. Before I could ask him what was going to happen to me, I was inside the cell; the metal gate swung closed and the realization sunk deep:

For the first time in my life I was no longer free.

* * *

I had no idea how long I slept, time as a measurable entity ceased to exist. The cell was small—about five feet tall, eight feet long and eight feet wide. I could never straighten up being taller than five feet. A faint light came from some place, enough to see vaguely the walls defining the cell. There was a cot inside it felt like it was made of metal with a blanket thrown across. Then I found, actually almost fell into, a round hole in one corner of the room about a half-foot in diameter, apparently for necessities, it smelled awfully foul.

Then there were rats.

Obnoxious aggressive rats in all sizes were running around on the floor, occasionally running up my legs at times inside my pants. I dragged the cot to the wall to the opposite side of the door, rolled myself into a ball and squeezed against the wall behind me.

The passing of time was deadly. For a while I started to count, got to around four thousand. There I lost count. Then I fell asleep until the rats came visiting. I became totally oblivious to time. I had no idea whether it was hours or days, maybe weeks. I thought maybe I was already dead. Time fell out of its dimension and eventually the place did as well. I tried to put some sense of reality into my head; the walls, the rats, and eventually my hunger; they were representing reality. Somewhere from another time zone came a voice, it felt like a voice traveling through infinite spaces.

"Ready to eat boy?"

First I thought it was Miska and began shaking uncontrollably.

But when he said: "Got some good bread for you, boy"—I realized that it was not him. He shoved a plate through the opening of the bars and left. *But why was he laughing?* There were two slices of rye bread on a wooden plate and a chunk of raw bacon. My hunger ruled, as mindlessly I began chewing on the bread first. I swallowed the first bite of it before the taste hit my palate. I spat whatever was still left in my mouth about ready to be swallowed; the bread was so salty that it did not taste like bread at all. It tasted like pure salt. Some of it glued to the roof of my mouth; I felt the skin inside my mouth shrinking. My throat became plugged with what felt like a salty gate, nothing going through, up or down. Something did: the leftover of half-digested food from God knows how long ago, combined with churning stomach acid headed upwards breaking through the salt gate. I was throwing up.

The thirst became simply unbearable.

My brain went into spasm, weird sick thoughts swirling like a winter storm trying to think of any moisture. Thoughts of everything: to grab a rat and bite his head off, suck his blood. The thought was so repulsive that I vomited some more. I suffered more than in all my life, barring none. I had no idea how much time passed before another guard came, opened the door and said:

"Follow me!"

I did gladly, wherever the trip would lead. If it's my execution I could no longer care. Let it be. After walking dark narrow stairways I guessed about three floors' worth, sunlight blinded me. We arrived from the catacombs. *Am I going to be dragged back again*, I wondered.

"QUESTIONING" said a sign on the door where the guard pushed me through. The room was on the street floor with narrowly paced iron bars on the outside of the window. Out there in the world it was daylight, the sun was somewhere on the other side of the building, judging from the intensity of the light, it had to be around mid-afternoon. The door opened and three AVO thugs came in, none of them in uniform. Subconsciously I felt that it would be somehow safer if they were in uniform. The underlying thought, however false it could have been, was, that the uniform would have represented some relevance to order, maybe some laws to abide by, perhaps even humanity.

The "questioning" was useless, totally unnecessary. They already knew every detail of my "adventure" but they were after a bigger fish.

I was the bait.

They needed me; rather they needed my confession.

The Communist "progress" was past the "promise land" stage; it was time for real action. They were to change the entire education system from the ground up. The parochial schools, (Premontre, Dominican, Jesuit, Benedictine) the breeding ground for educating kids in capitalist morals had to be shot down. Even though they already had the power to do that, it was still a risky move, the biggest yet in the takeover. They needed an excuse and I provided a handy one. Well known in the school with a rising popularity in my boxing career and caught in undeniable circumstances of an obvious and admitted escape attempt to Austria; all neatly wrapped up, with one small piece missing: a written and signed confession.

There it was, in front of the shortest, most civilized looking thug, dark rimmed glasses, long sleeve shirt, definitely the best dressed one. I could see the confession easily, maybe six feet away from my eyes. But there was something else on the table they just placed there: a pitcher of water, with perspiring small beads of water rolling down on the side of the pitcher, indicating ice cold water inside.

The scene was surreal.

I was sitting at the end of the long table; the three AVO operatives occupied the remaining three sides. Three items were on the table: a typed one page confession, a pitcher of ice cold water and an empty glass. Real glass, clean, sparkling, empty. Maybe crystal. The AVO agent with the confession in front of him flashed a smile:

"You want to read it or just sign it. We don't care, you should not either, it won't matter anyway." He pushed the confession in front of me.

My thirst was beyond description. My eyes were riveted at the pitcher, the water looked like a body coming alive, softly undulating from side to side, became waves of an ocean, although I never had seen an ocean, only in pictures. But I was convinced that this was now an ocean in front of me, inviting me to dive in. Shakespeare's "My kingdom for a horse" came to mind in a "My life for a glass of water" version.

The "confession" was of no surprise. Typed in a rather primitive language with more typos than any teacher would ever let a student get by with, simply stating that I, then the inserted name of the accused, was in the process of escaping to Austria carrying a message to the Austrian bishop of Graz, describing terror, mayhem, and other kinds of atrocities committed by the Communists against the priests of the school and asking for help from the Imperialists (i.e.: the Americans) stationed west of Austria, West Germany. I also had to state in the confession that I clearly knew that the accusations were lies, but the school's headmaster pursued me to comply. It was pure fabrication, every single word of it, but my signature would make it believable, at least to those who needed to be convinced.

Something unbelievable happened: I became two persons. One sitting there staring at the water, the other one walking out of my body and slowly strolling around the table. That other me stopped at the opposite end of the table, looked at me with a strange curious look and spoke to me. I could never recall exactly what he said, but his voice was calm, his throat was clear. He spoke of values, spoke of time infinitum, spoke of God in all of us, spoke of eternal love, and eternal peace. I had never heard such a voice before; it filled the whole room, sometimes echoed, other times it was far away and again in front of me, like being me.

An incredible out of body experience.

That other me now was coming around. His slowly swinging arm touched the shoulders of each AVO men, softly stroking them. They, one by one, dropped their head, bowing their chins toward their chests. Then the other me got to the guy with the confession page: he held his arm gently as he now began pouring water into the glass. It kept pouring and pouring, never seemed to end. Then this "other me" pushed the water close to the confession paper and with a soft, gentle sweep of his arm tipped the glass of water over. It looked so casual, almost like an accident.

My out of body experience came to an end.

I realized that I was the one, me, the real me who knocked over the glass. The water was now flowing over the confession, obliterating the typewritten words, as they floated into a small lake of black inky water.

I expected to be beaten to pulp, but again, life always has its surprises. Two of them stepped outside of the room and after a few minutes one of them came back and turned to me:

"The guard will take you back into your cell. You'll get food and water and brought back here in a week. I am sure you'll be more careful with the water in front of you then. A lot more careful." He said all these as a matter of fact, but there was something frightening and ominous tone in those calm words. As he stepped away the guard came around and grabbed my arm.

Surprisingly less than a day later they let me go. I was imprisoned for over two days. As I learned years later, the school headmaster was arrested and due to the third degree interrogation, he confessed to any and all crimes he was accused of.

My confession was no longer needed.

TWO HUNDRED FIFTEEN...
TWO HUNDRED SIXTEEN...

I LOVED TO WRITE: POEMS AND SHORT STORIES MOSTLY. After graduation I applied for admission to the University of Literary Sciences in Budapest. I was determined to be a journalist.

My application was rejected. At first I could not believe it. I should have been THE perfect candidate. Coming from a real proletariat background, which by then became prerequisite for admission to any university, graduated from high school with high grades, spoke three languages, even got published. There had to be some mistake.

I went to see the head of the Admissions Advisory Committee by then under the control of the Party and was told that I was accepted to the University of Chemical Engineering in Veszprem.

"But I never applied for that!" I was indignant.

Well, I was told, either to become a chemist, or no university. After all, the newly-instituted socialist economic phenomenon, the Five-Year Plan, needed chemical engineers, not poets.

"Won't you agree, comrade?" asked the man who met me.

Shove your Five-Year Plan, I thought to myself and walked out.

Screw the university, let's get a job instead! and I did, a relatively lucrative one in the construction business. Nevertheless when application time came around next year, my father begged me to apply for admission.

Reluctantly I did submit my admission request to both the University of Literary Sciences in Budapest, as well as to the University of Chemical Engineering in Veszprem for the fall semester of September 1951. A few weeks later when I got home, my father handed me an envelope. I expected it to be my acceptance to either of the universities.

Surprise, surprise!

It was from the Army. Enclosed were my induction papers, instructing me to report for duty the following Wednesday. I was devastated. The Hungarian Red Army was as bad as a prison. Serving four years, at some God-forgotten eastern Hungarian border post, four years stolen out of my life. Yet I knew that there was no way to escape serving in the Hungarian Red Army, except one: being enrolled in a university. University students were exempt from military service, largely because part of the curriculum was military training, and during summer breaks there was a mandatory four weeks active military duty. But for me now, a potential admission to any university was months away, the induction into the Army was less than a week.

As always, when in a corner, I developed a plan, and as usual, Plan One was backed by Plan Two. Plan One was to visit Julius and ask for whatever influence he could use to help me delay my induction date. As a rule, the AVO had a lot of power, but the visit was not easy. Julius was already an AVO officer, albeit still low rank, but he was hard to reach simply because he was AVO. Another problem was my pride. Julius was fast climbing the ladder to the top hierarchy of the AVO, he no longer considered me a friend. I swallowed my pride, went to see the guard at the AVO headquarters, he told me to come back a week later. Induction time was next Wednesday and thus Plan One, short-lived as it was, suffered its premature death.

It was time for Plan Two.

Every weekend there was a boxing competition match within the district. On the following Sunday the match was to be against the Celldomolk team. I worked up a "plan". I had to be knocked out whether for real or have a fake concussion, get myself to a hospital, the only temporary haven from the Army, and somehow manage to stay in the hospital until my admission would come from the university. It no longer mattered from which one.

Three months in a mental hospital, but first I had to get there!

It was easier to design a plan than to carry it out. First, I had to be actually knocked out, something that never happened before. Amidst the booing of a half-packed gymnasium, I did manage it by literally walking into my opponent, Bergi's right hand and finally this time for real, down I went. The next day my coach, concerned about proclaimed symptoms, took me to the Szombathely hospital for examination, wherein came the rest of my problems.

What were the symptoms of a real concussion, which I did not actually have?

To blink or not to blink when the examining doctor, who happened to be head of the psychiatry department, Dr. Tanka, flashed light into my pupils? To react or not to react when the sharp needle scratched the bottom of my feet? After about fifteen minutes Dr. Tanka finished his examination and sat down.

"Now can you tell me the real problem?"

I was sure I flunked the exam. I knew that as a last resort I had to come up with an answer, with any answer, other than the truth. I was searching desperately every cavity of my brain for an answer, until out of nowhere, surfaced one.

"Doctor, it's actually a small matter, but I need help. Inside my head there are three monkeys and two chairs. The monkeys fight for the chairs, driving me crazy. To stop the fight, you either put one more chair into my head or take one monkey out!"

Dr. Tanka looked at me a long time with penetrating, icy blue eyes, then said slowly,

"I think we can take care of the problem."

I was admitted to the hospital's psychiatric ward. When I did not show up for induction, the Army went to my parents' home. They were told that I was in the hospital. The same day, the Army showed up at the hospital where Dr. Tanka informed them that I had suffered a serious concussion that would require lengthy treatment as an inpatient at the hospital. The Army left, and I spent the next three months in the psychiatric ward. In late August I learned that I was accepted to the University of Chemical Engineering. I went to Veszprem directly from the hospital.

I never learned whether Dr. Tanka ever realized what I was up to, but I could reasonably assume that the visit by the Army gave him a hint.

"Those wonderful icy blue eyes!" I remembered now.

TWO HUNDRED FORTY-TWO...
TWO HUNDRED FORTY-THREE...

GENUINELY DISLIKED CHEMISTRY. My high school education was so superior that I continued to breeze through the exams with little difficulty, mostly with A's. I also continued my martial arts training without a sensei, practicing Kung Fu and some aikido for an hour or more a day. Martial arts were not part of the curriculum at the university.

It was at the first exam when I got an unexpected break.

The entire 1951 student body, about 500 students, was divided into four sections around 125 students each based on the various disciplines of chemistry and then again into four subsections of 30 students each. These units were called, "study circles". For most students math represented the fear of all fears. It was the first exam of the semester. In the preceding weeks the preparation by the students had been furious. We were told that the exam would be conducted by the head of the faculty, Laszlo Toth, who was as famous for his uncompromising demand for a student's knowledge of math as he was for his pioneering mathematical theories. My study circle was well prepared, or so they thought after endless nights of study sessions, doing mock exams, solving hypothetical problems. I did not participate in the collective prep work, not for any particular reason; I was not exceptionally good in math, but I just had no interest in group activities.

"A tell-tale sign of anti-social, anti-collectivist behavior," I was told by some party zealot.

Then the day came for the exam. It was conducted in alphabetical order, which placed me at number 13. There were twelve students ahead of me.

The twelve got reduced to nine, which moved me up to number ten.

This is what happened.

Professor Toth had flunked the first nine exam takers in a row. Numbers 10, 11 and 12 panicked and vanished. Terror reigned. Word got around fast, and by the time my turn came, the exam room that usually had no more than those taking the exam—maybe 30 or so—was now filled to capacity. At least a hundred students were jammed in the room to watch the slaughter, some out of curiosity, others with fear enveloping their hearts because their exam time was yet to come. The math problem I was given to solve was neither easy nor exceptionally difficult just a bit "tricky". But there was something about the problem that struck me. First, I was sure that once, somewhere in the past I had faced solving this, or a very similar problem, but had no idea when and where. The second thing that struck me was that there was more than one approach to solve: a standard, by-the-book solution and an unusual, a so-called elegant solution, the one that I seemed to know by heart. As I was setting up the unorthodox equation to solve the problem, the room got silent. Professor Toth suddenly showed an unusual interest, as if he hoped I would fail.

I almost did.

I easily danced through solving the problem. In the final stage I had to multiply three by three and kept coming up with eight repeatedly. I just could not see it! I began to perspire.

Then a voice, as if it had come from a distant planet, reached me.

"A rather unusual but elegant solution, an A+, just remember that three by three is still nine."

Laughter in the room, the exam became the talk of the class for days to come.

For me a handicap in the long run.

TWO HUNDRED SIXTY-TWO...
TWO HUNDRED SIXTY-THREE...

THE SEMESTERS PROGRESSED, THE EASY PASSING OF EXAMS GOT TO MY HEAD. There were times when I was totally unprepared and flunked, then went on a quick study drill of three or four sleepless nights and usually got an "A" at the repeat exam. But the quickly learned knowledge disappeared just as fast. Later on when it was needed as a base of future studies, I no longer had it. I should have known that my arrogance and lack of serious studying would come back to haunt me.

The supervisor of the mandatory lab work was Eva, the daughter of a well-known professor. From day one we had a mutual dislike for one another, for whatever reason, she hated me. To pass I needed to excel, which I did not. At the end of the fifth semester, three semesters short of graduating, I flunked lab. No repeat test on lab practices. I had to repeat the entire year. I was in too much of a hurry with life to do that. By then some of my writings began to appear in the local newspaper, and as far as I was concerned, chemistry was not my destiny anyway. I considered the fiasco as God's intervention saving me from becoming a chemist, from being an obedient cog in the Communist agenda for the benefit of the almighty state.

But leave the university and then go where? To do what?

I decided to appeal for help from Manny, trying to stay at the university without losing a year. His name was Marton Mandel; everybody called him Manny. He was handicapped: he had a shorter right leg and it seemed with every step that he forgot to move it, then suddenly remembered and dragged it. He had a well-built upper body, wide shoulders, with a big head sticking away from his shoulders, held at a very slight, but visibly tilted angle.

Manny came to the university from the eastern part of Hungary, from a small city called Cegled. He was a bit older than the rest of us in the class, maybe by three or four years. Prior to arrival at the university he must have been a party apparatchik, a small functionary of the Communist Party. He seemed not only to know the rules set by the Party, he also lived by them. Manny was the secretary of the student body's Communist Party, wielding huge influence as to what was to happen to students before and after graduation. He was a better than mediocre student, he was in my "study circle". Earlier on I caught Manny's attention, because in spite of being the study group leader preparing for the math exam in those early days, he barely passed.

"Why don't you come to one of our party initiation meetings?" he asked me one day after my famous math A+ act: "I am sure you'd like what you hear…"

"I'll try," I told him with little enthusiasm, but I didn't. Manny never asked me again. Now it was my time to ask Manny for help.

The gods were not in my favor that day.

I went to his office. He was busy, so I had to sit in the small lobby. The door was closed but the argument inside the office was loud and aggravated, and I could easily hear every word.

"I don't care if he got the Nobel Prize in physics! He is not going to question, let alone to criticize, the Party's directives laid down by the Central Committee and Comrade Rakosi himself. Who the hell does he think he is?"

The voice sounded familiar. I recognized the outburst being that of Eddy Lantos, the Agitprop Secretary of the Veszprem Regional District Communist Party. That particular body was in charge of life and death and everybody—Manny for sure—knew it. Obviously he was on the defensive, condescending.

"Comrade Lantos, Dr. Bender did not mean to criticize the party line. He is a member of the Party and a recipient of the coveted Stalin Award in…"

Lantos never let him finish.

"Stalin Award or no Stalin Award," he said, and then realized that he may have gone too far too soon. Stalin was dead for less than a year and nobody knew what direction the Kremlin's line was heading. He may still be a demigod in his death, but words were floating around that the Generalissimo may have already fallen from grace.

Lantos retreated:

"I don't mean to belittle the award named after our great leader, but Dr. Bender has to realize that the Party is the ultimate rule maker, regardless. Just tell him to stay with thermodynamics and keep his opinion about Marxism-Leninism to himself."

Then he stormed out, walked by, never even looked at me. Obviously Dr. Bender spoke out of Party line, somewhere feeling safe making questionable remarks. *What a fool!*

Manny came out of his office, but instead of inviting me inside, positioned himself against the doorway, leaning into the doorframe, slowly dragging his right foot forward as if assuming a fighting stance.

"So Eva flunked you, eh?"

Bad news travels fast, I thought and nodded.

"Yep, she sure did."

"You've never been her favorite," Manny said, as if offering sympathy, but I knew better. Sympathy was not included in his portfolio. I started to regret being there now, begging the mercy of this Party monster I never liked, too late now. So I told myself: *bite the bullet*.

"You never had much use for this university," Manny began his lecture. Still leaning against the doorframe, balancing so well one would never know about his shorter right leg. His stance seemed to give him more confidence as he went on.

"What are you doing here anyway, flashing your arrogance from day one? What makes you think you are different? Acting as if this great institution was created for your exclusive personal pleasure?"

"Have you got any idea why we"—now he was getting rather imperial, I thought, as he switched to the royal we—"built this university here in this hick town?"

He did not seem to care for my answer as he was on full throttle.

"So that we can break the back of the damned church, that's why! The Archbishop of Veszprem was the most powerful of bishops. After we extracted Cardinal Mindszenty, this city became the last bastion of their whole religious empire. Yeah, that was what they thought, an empire 'til we decided to wipe it out without using force. We used you and hundreds of the likes of you!"

His stance became more solid. He leaned forward, his right arm was lifted, his right index finger pointed at me like a lance.

"Hundreds," he said again, "but not really like you. We did not break the church to replace it with the arrogance of the individual and the likes of you. The Party does not need your flashing individualism, your elegant math solutions. The Party does not need you, period. We need soldiers, nameless, faceless soldiers. The Party does not care about your ambitions. It is not designed to please your agenda."

Now Manny took a deep breath. He must have become tired of his fighting stance. He began to walk away back to the inner office. I did not know whether the diatribe was over, whether I was invited inside or not. I decided to follow him anyway. He turned around at his desk, leaned against it still standing as he continued.

"Do you know how Comrade Stalin handled those standing in the way of the Party's objectives?"

I could have given a few examples myself, but decided to let him ramble on, mostly out of curiosity. I may even find out what the latest Party line is after the death of the world's highest ranked train robber; never hurts to know. Stalin might be sliding from grace and Manny may already know it.

Let him tell.

But Manny apparently changed his mind about Stalin's contributions to history—like three million Tatars in box cars to the Gulags, the deliberate starving of seven million Ukrainians in 1933, the murdering of hundreds and thousands of his ex-comrades-in-arms, the list was endless.

Manny's final words were directed straight at me.

"I cannot help you. Even if I could, I would not. You don't belong here. The Party does not need you. Those who build socialism don't need you. Now get out of my office. Get out of this university, and if you have any good common sense, get out of town."

He turned around, made a firm step with his left foot dragged the right behind and not even wasting another look at me, sat down. With a wave of his right hand I was dismissed.

His words kept echoing "get out of town!" I wondered why Manny stopped short of suggesting for me to *"get out of the country..."* Hmm.

***

The summer was still young when I arrived at Pecs, the third largest and most beautiful city in Hungary, a breath of fresh air after Veszprem. Eva with her lab class, Manny with his sermon all seemed light-years away.

The breeze came off of a mountain called Mecsek, spreading over the northeast end of the city. The wind brought scent of the late blooming acacia tree flowers.

I needed a lucky break.

Unbeknownst to me, it was already in the making.

Ever since the Communists forced the Hungarian farmers into the state owned co-ops around 1950-51, the agricultural productivity of the land had taken a steady decline. By 1953 the crop was so disastrous that the country, once one of the food baskets of Europe, was struck by famine. The industrial sector was hurting the most. Csepel, the famous "Craddle of the Red Proletariat", where the steel and other factories were located, was in a state of near-riot.

The Hungarian peasants struck back. They decided to sabotage their oppressors' plan.

The Party tried everything: intimidation, terror, imprisonment, even indiscriminate executions. "The works" by the real pros of the AVO.

Nothing worked. The food supply kept declining. The Central Committee, after receiving Moscow's approval, decided that it was time for Lenin's Two-Steps-Forward-One-Step-Backward strategy.

This time it was the step backward from socialist progress.

Late in 1953 a new Party directive was issued declaring that a certain percentage of all productive farmland be returned into private ownership and the farmers were allowed to bring the crops grown on that privately owned land to the free market place. To re-establish credibility, Imre Nagy, member of the old-guard Communist faction was elevated to the position of Prime Minister. He had the physical profile of a typical Hungarian farmer: high forehead, wide cheekbones, rolling handlebar mustache, a voice that roared and supposedly spoke the truth. The Party knew that the Hungarian peasants trusted Nagy, and credibility by then was a rare and precious commodity. Installing him as the Prime Minister was supposed to deliver that credibility. The food supply had to be doubled to avoid or at least to delay disaster.

New fresh political winds were blowing and people were re-invigorated with long lost hopes. I went to the editorial offices of the Dunantuli Naplo, a regional daily paper and asked to see the head of the agricultural department. Agriculture became a coveted segment of the economy and consequently considerable party-directed media interest. The editor of the department was Emery Oroszlan, a name that translates into "lion". His appearance lived up to his name. He had a narrow face, a cat-like mouth and nose, which seemed to come to a focal point in the center of his face. His head was crowned by a bushy mane that definitely would have made his namesake proud.

Oroszlan cut to the chase quickly:

"Any samples of your writings? Anything published?"

I handed over a folder with a few of my best articles from Veszprem, heavily edited by the Party's Agitprop division. Oroszlan scanned it, then opined, "You probably write better than this," as his words trailed off. I knew that I was dealing with a true survivor.

"Come in tomorrow," Oroszlan said, "Szamoca will drive you to Mohacs. There is a kolhoz about to break up. Hot stuff, don't screw up!"

I did not.

The collective farm did in fact break apart that night, revealing lots of deep-seated anger. The meeting came close to a fistfight. The story was ripe for telling. I finished the article that night, working into the wee hours of the morning, dropped it off at Oroszlan's desk, went to my small apartment, slept a couple of hours and went back to his office, trying to see him. He was not available. He was in meetings. Or maybe it was just an excuse. I was nervous all day and the next morning I anxiously picked up a copy of the paper. There it was a major feature, the entire article virtually unedited! The next day when I saw Oroszlan, he shook my hand and simply said:

"Welcome aboard!"

Newspapers in Hungary, or for that matter in the entire Soviet Block, were under the tightest control of the Communist Party Central Committee. The Party was fully aware of the power of the media, the Fourth Estate. The publisher of every newspaper in the country was also the Secretary of the District Committee. There were thirteen District Committees in Hungary. Alas, there were thirteen newspapers in the country plus one: The *Szabad Nep* (*The Free People*) for the whole country, published by the Central Committee of the Communist Party. To read the Free People was mandatory. At each working place, whether it was a large factory, a small manufacturing place, or an office of any size, every working shift was preceded by 20-minute indoctrination. The Party rep read the paper aloud (if he/she was illiterate, someone was delegated to do so) and all the "children" of the State were required to listen with undivided attention. The reader would conclude the session with, "Long live Socialism and our beloved father, Stalin."

I convinced myself that the Party had come to an understanding of the value of individual incentive and the country was getting on the right track, toward some form of limited freedom. The "Dunantuli Naplo" was a newspaper, like the other twelve, composed of four pages. The front page consisted of international news as interpreted or sanitized by the Kremlin, released by TASS, the Soviet wire service, copied by MTI, the Hungarian wire service, and picked up by thirteen newspapers.

Page two had editorials composed every day by the Central Committee in Budapest and approved by the office of the Kremlin's watchman, the Soviet Ambassador to Hungary. Page four was sports, entertainment, trivia. But part of page three for local feature stories, interviews, politic in the district could occasionally, I believed, become mine!

What a misperception that was!

By the end of 1954 the privately owned land in Hungary produced more food than the remaining much larger collectively cultivated segment, the kolhoz. The Communists saved the country from a famine-induced rebellion, I took great pride in being a small part of the success. The Communist Party, after the goal of producing the necessary food was accomplished, no longer needed the private sector, and was ready to strike back at the peasantry. It was time for Lenin's "two steps forward" strategy.

In the meantime, something monumental happened in my life: I fell in love.

TWO HUNDRED NINETY-FIVE...
TWO HUNDRED NINETY-SIX...

THE PLANE APPARENTLY ENCOUNTERED MINOR TURBULENCE; IT DROPPED SLIGHTLY FORWARD ONLY TO JERK BACK INTO A LEVELED FLIGHT. Anais turned her head suddenly—perhaps an involuntary reflex reaction. It had been agreed that we all act as strangers and not even look at each other or communicate once on board, but, I now found ourselves momentarily exchanging glances.

Her huge dark eyes seemed to float in the swells of an ocean of emotions. I had no way of deciphering it. *Was it love? Was it fear? Was it the sail of a ship carrying the last message of our lives? Was it the final goodbye?*

The slide projector of my life slid back eighteen months.

***

The snow was falling at Pecs. The top of Mecsek Mountain had a white cap as if someone had crowned its venerable head with a white yarmulke.

It was the winter of 1954-55, a year of another round of dramatic changes in Hungary. The socialist, collectivist brainwashing program, designed to elevate the cultural level of the proletariat, did not seem to get any traction despite six years of extensive Communist re-education. Sure, all forms of bourgeois art were banned, whether it was music, poetry, theater or film. In 1954 the much heralded "rebirth of socialist cultural revival" was still in the first trimester of its "pregnancy" and seemed to be stalled there for good.

Just as well.

The former feudal state of Hungary, with less than seven million residents, produced more giants in the field of art and science in the 19th and 20th centuries than any other nation with a comparable or even much larger population. Just consider a few of the several hundreds: Liszt, Bartok, Kodaly, Munkacsy, Szilard, Teller; the list is virtually endless. In contrast, all the new Communist Cultural Revolution could produce were enthusiastic marching songs.

"*We march and fight for the peace of the proletariat, we produce more wheat than anyone else*"... "*The Red Csepel is ready to go to war for the liberation and the peace of the proletariat of the world*" and so it went on, and on, and on; the rehashed adulation of schmaltzy marching songs fashioned after their equally primitive Soviet counterparts. Passages such as "*marching for the victory of the Party, led by our father the great Stalin,*" were simply translated into Hungarian from Russian.

By 1954, the Party had its hands full with a lot more to worry about than new marching songs, or love poetry promoting the ultimate victory of the oppressed masses of the capitalist world. Dealing with famine while trying to control the excesses that somehow allotted capitalism to sneak back with that ugly idea called "individual incentive," a purely bourgeois phenomenon of course, required all of the resources the Party had. In addition, the loosening of Party disciplines, the conflicting signals from Moscow, the lack of adequate rules to govern the "proletariat masses" all combined to create a vacuum into which decadent capitalist habits and practices were creeping back.

Like jazz.

On a narrow side street off Nador Square in Pecs, there was a nondescript doorway, halfway between two marble columns left over from another era. A hand-painted sign declared nothing about the place except its name, THE STUDIO. Inside the double glass doors was the best New Orleans jazz on the east side of the Iron Curtain. It was my favored hangout in late evenings. I loved jazz. I knew that jazz was not on the Central Committee's list of approved entertainment, but really, I could not care less. I was an avant-garde reporter successfully promoting the present Party line. I assumed jazz would be, if not accepted, probably tolerated by the hierarchy of the Party, at least for the time being. And the Party might take the attitude I took: could not care less.

At THE STUDIO, a musician by the name of Duli played the sax. After a few visits we became friends. Duli admitted to being an expatriate from Budapest, no details though. Many nights we spent the breaks of the band together, usually 15 or 20 minutes, three times a night.

It was one night in early 1955. At about ten o'clock, as usual, I walked into the dimly lit place. It was quiet, the first break of the night for the music. There were four musicians on four instruments: sax, guitar, bass and drum.

As my eyes adjusted to the darkness, I saw Duli sitting at our favorite table with two women. He was sitting with his back toward the door, so he did not see me. I hesitated; I had considered it "our table" but I was not sure whether or not it was proper to butt in. Then something stopped me in my hesitant tracks. One woman, I guessed to be the older of the two, although I could only see her in half-profile, was talking to

Duli. But the other one! Wow! She was facing the door, looking right at me. My immediate reaction was:

"Oh my God!"

It was her eyes, I realized, that stopped me. Two black diamonds, brilliantly sparkling in a perfectly shaped oval face framed by a rich crown of jet-black hair…

The eyes.

I did not remember ever seeing eyes like that, yet they were for some reason so familiar, as if I had seen them all my life. Duli, maybe sensing my presence, stopped talking and turned around.

"Hey Zak," he said as he noticed me staring, "let me introduce!" He did. The two women were relatives. The older one was the wife of the Director General of the Pecs Hospital, a well-known physician. Her niece was from the northeastern part of Hungary.

She had black diamonds for eyes and Anais for a name. Her father was mayor of a small city, Ujfeherto (New White Lake) before the Communists took over. He was now branded a "kulak", a Russian name for the undesirable peasant, one who owned any amount of land. He was saved from deportation—at least for a while—simply because he was probably the kindest, fairest man in the entire district and the Socialist Revolution's class cleansing act was yet to be fully completed.

I learned most of that during my visit with them that night.

The music started after a while and I stayed as Duli went back to his sax. There was small-talk for the rest of the night, mostly by the aunt. Neither Anais nor I seemed to hear a single word, as if an electromagnetic shield had been created, blocking everything but our desire to be with one another. It was suddenly an unspoken agreement for everything to be blocked out of the world other than ours. Time seemed to fly. It came close to midnight, curfew time for the two women. They were at THE STUDIO only because Anais wanted to hear live jazz for the first time.

"Are you coming back here again?" I asked, as they were getting ready to leave. While I asked them both obviously the question was really directed at Anais. She looked at her aunt as if for permission. The aunt shrugged her shoulder, Anais turned to me.

"Someday I am sure we will!" The words were non-committal, but the eyes, those black diamond eyes were signaling:

"Oh, yes! Oh, yes, I will!"

That night, as I went home, I knew that love has arrived in my life.

***

Yes, she was there at THE STUDIO a few nights later and the night after that and the night after that. A few weeks later, Duli was blasting out Chattanooga Choo-Choo on the sax when she turned to me. Her voice was unusually low, husky, "Do you want to spend the night with me?"

We took the streetcar to the part of town where I lived. I had to go to work the next morning, and as we woke up, I still felt her body's vibration from the passion that took over our lives, our entire existence, making love all night with no end in sight.

It was early. I was sitting on the side of the bed dressing when she spoke.

"I was thinking last night. If we make love, I can't wear a white wedding dress when we get married. Hmmm, I thought. Then I kind of mentally inventoried my wardrobe at home, and I realized that I don't even have a white dress. On top of that, you never asked to marry me anyway, did you?"

THREE HUNDRED FIFTEEN...
THREE HUNDRED SIXTEEN...

T
HE PLANE WAS NOW HUMMING SOFTLY, THE FLIGHT WAS SMOOTH
AND ANAIS WAS NO LONGER LOOKING AT ME. I felt a huge void as
I looked at her just three seats ahead on the opposite side of the
aisle. The void was growing into an ever-widening canyon that might
never be bridged again.

Guilt came upon me like a grizzly bear clawing at my soul with
heavy claws.

*Why did I bring her on this life-or-death or more likely, death-or-life
journey? Why did she have to face almost sure rape, torture and eventually
death at the hands of the thugs of the AVO? Why did I marry her in the first
place? I was already on the run, hiding from place to place. Why? Just for
the zest of love? Throwing a beautiful young life away?* As the countdown
approached the end, I was, from moment to moment, more convinced
that the plan would not work.

149

Impossible, impossible! A cacophony of inaudible voices were loudly screaming in my head. *I must tell George that we should abort,* but of course I knew that it was impossible. It was too late for that; the race for life or death had to be finished.

Alea iacta est my demons answered with their laughs. *The dice have been rolled.*

All I wished now was just to be somewhere in a place of nothingness, maybe back at Pecs, the night that we spent together, so that I could put my arms around her, just one more time. That I could seal her lips with mine, just one more time. That we could have the incredible joy of making love, just one more time. And as we were making love, just let the plane crash, never coming back into reality again. Just one more time for a never-ending second. I had to wipe my cheek with the back of my hand as the salty taste of a lonely tear slowly traveled down, reaching the corner of my mouth.

Just one more time!

THREE HUNDRED TWENTY...
THREE HUNDRED TWENTY-ONE...

T WAS SPRING, 1955. Although the newspaper provided me with a car and a driver, a privilege afforded only to dignitaries in Hungary, I was allowed to use the car only for traveling to locations for stories. I sub-rented an apartment and usually took the electric streetcar to the office in the morning. The closest stop of the streetcar to the newspaper office was about 200 yards past, and to save the walking back from the station, I usually jumped off the streetcar's open platform as it passed the office at a very low speed.

One morning as usual I was about to jump off, when something stopped me. My eyes caught the sight of two Pobeda, a luxury vehicle reserved for the Communist Party's elite. I had not seen those cars around the office before.

My atavistic senses smelled danger. I stayed on the streetcar all the way to the end station, got off and then walked up Mecsek Mountain to a small coffee shop on the top. I ordered a poppy seed cake, coffee and then listened to the radio.

I learned before noon that my senses were right. According to the broadcast, the Prime Minister, Imre Nagy, was kicked out of the Party: his agenda was declared detrimental to the interest of the People's Republic of Hungary. (Later, in 1956, he was arrested, sentenced to death and in 1958 he was executed). The broadcast further stated that several hundreds of Nagy's "accomplices" were also arrested, many of whom had "infiltrated the media" and future arrests were being planned. My lucky star had fallen.

The hunt was on and I became the hunted.

THREE HUNDRED THIRTY-SIX...
THREE HUNDRED THIRTY-SEVEN

N 1954, AT ABOUT 600 FEET ALTITUDE, A SOVIET MILITARY TRANSPORT PLANE GOT LOST IN LOW CLOUD COVER AND FLEW SMACK INTO THE HILLSIDE NORTHWEST OF PECS, OVER A SMALL VILLAGE CALLED KOVAGOSZOLOS. Soviet military personnel went on a routine mission to investigate the cause of the crash. Then some strange things started to happen. Pecs was of no strategic importance to the Russians; until the crash of the plane, only token Russian troops were stationed in some old WWII army barracks.

But now a flurry of activities took place.

Military troop movements could be seen day after day. Lines of canvas-covered Soviet military trucks were moving up into the hills. Night after night, heavy construction equipment was heading the same way. In less than a month, an area of the hillside covering several hundred acres was surrounded with electrically charged barbed-wire fencing and became forbidden territory for local Hungarians. Armed Russian troops were guarding every road, trail, and walkway leading up the hill. Powerful searchlights were set up to scan the night. Looking from Pecs northwest, where a month ago one could see only flickering lights, now rose a mysterious city basking in floodlights, illuminating the sky for miles to see. Then some of the Russians left, and one day a convoy of canvas-covered trucks brought in hundreds of men.

Hungarians. Military units mixed with political prisoners all dressed in military garb. By now everybody knew the "well-kept" secret: the Russians by accident had discovered a rich uranium field, containing high-yield, high-quality uranium (U238), the most important ingredient for producing nuclear weapons.

The Russians already had a cover name for the mines: EXPEDITION TWO.

THREE HUNDRED FIFTY-TWO...
THREE HUNDRED FIFTY-THREE...

THE OPTIONS I HAD TO SURVIVE THE "CLEANSING OF THE IMPERIALIST ELEMENTS" WERE LIMITED. IN A LAND WHERE EVERY PERSON'S LIFE IS FULLY CONTROLLED BY THE GOVERNMENT, THERE ARE VERY FEW PLACES TO HIDE. The "elimination of the enemies of Socialism" was in progress. I needed to explore ways to escape Hungary, to avoid a likely imprisonment, or maybe worse, who knows. I made arrangements to meet someone by the name of Andy.

He was quite a character, a bit on the shady side. I met him at THE STUDIO; he was a steady patron of the place. He claimed to have several "evocations" as he called them, including being a fisherman. Andy used to drive his beaten up Puch motorcycle to Mohacs, a city on the west bank of the Danube, to fish. He also claimed to be a human smuggler helping Hungarians escape to Yugoslavia via the Danube. Actually, such escape was moving from one slavery to another, with Marshall Tito, a

Communist dictator ruling Yugoslavia, successfully resisting the political dictates of Moscow. But there was one major difference: no Iron Curtain separated Yugoslavia from Italy, offering a better chance of escaping to the West. I planned to meet Andy that night. I left a message for him with his mother to meet me at a restaurant called Rose Garden at nine o'clock that evening.

I arrived early. A band of three gypsies was playing soft dancing music when I entered. The restaurant was a romantic, offbeat place. It had a garden with huge oak trees and rosebushes adjacent to the building, just as its name proclaimed. It was a warm spring night; the garden area was open for customers. I walked in, looking around for the darkest spot. By this evening, my life had become totally different from what it was only a day before. It was a strange feeling of "being on the run." My eyes swept the place from side to side, searching for predators. None seemed to be around and even if they were, I would not know how to spot them, would not know what to look for.

Two tables away from where I finally settled, a couple was sitting. The man seemed to be in his forties, he was wearing a pair of expensive-looking, thin, gold-rimmed glasses. A woman, his date, looked half his age, pretty. Another table away sat three young men in their twenties. They were drinking red wine heavily and getting more rowdy by the liters.

Punks, I thought. I hated punks.

All afternoon I was considering my options. There weren't many. Judged by the news, the purge was already in full swing. Hundreds, perhaps thousands of "conspirators" were now under arrest. Fear was like a cloud descending on the land. For me, to surface by going back to the paper was no longer an option. I was considered to be one of the so-called "conspirators," even if only a small-timer. Escape to Yugoslavia had a remote chance of success, but that was the only one I had and I needed to know as much as was possible about it. Hence the meeting set with Andy.

It was already past nine. No sign of him.

I kept watching the door for his arrival. In the meantime, from the corner of my eye I saw trouble brewing. The punks were drunk and were eyeing the table of the couple, more specifically the young woman at the table. Based on my experience with behavior of drunken punks, I knew that there was definitely going to be an unpleasant maybe violent encounter.

Come on Andy, get here! This trouble is too close! I don't want to be part of it!

There was no sign of him.

Now one of the punks got up, walked over to the couple's table, conducting what appeared to be a polite conversation, most likely asking her to dance.

She smiled but shook her head. The intruder shrugged his shoulders and walked back to the table where the two others were laughing loudly at him.

Still, no Andy.

A few minutes passed, and when another one of the punks got up, walked toward the couple's table, I knew that this time trouble had fully arrived. The outside street gate was to my left, the couple's table to my right, the table of the three drunks beyond that.

I was considering the available scenarios.

Get up and leave. No, I can't do that. I did not pay for the glass of wine yet, Andy may still be coming—the meeting is too important to abandon.

Let the fight go on. For sure there will be one. Not my problem, especially not now. Stay put!

No, I can't do that either. These three punks will eat that poor guy alive.

I was also sizing him up as he arrived at the couple's table. Clumsy body movements it looked rather unlikely that he ever had any fighting experience.

How about my own? I felt good about it. I practiced my kata-s every day for at least an hour. To honor my black belt status I made it a mandatory routine.

Still…maybe I should go over there attempting to defuse the situation?

It was too late. The argument had already started at the couple's table. The second punk was turned down as well, but this one was not taking no for an answer. The rest happened too fast, yet appeared to proceed in slow motion.

The punk reached for the woman's arm as the frail-looking man stood up, protesting. He was moving around to protect the woman, blocking the way of the intruder. The punk launched a quick, unexpected punch. He missed the intended target halfway, but connected with the man's glasses, they dropped to the floor. The man without his glasses seemed to be disoriented.

My options expired. It took me four steps.

I tapped the punk on the shoulder. He was slightly taller, a perfect target. With a surprised face he spun around and as I expected, launched a really lousy, wobbly right. Now that was a real amateur move; I knew I had him. It was now my choice how much punishment I wanted to, maybe had to—considering there were two more of them—administer.

My main training was in Kung Fu, but I did a considerable amount of Aikido as well. The punk who did not have good balance to begin with, was relatively drunk and wobbly, he turned around too fast, and had thrown a punch way off-target.

A dream for an Aikido move.

I expected the right, so as it came I leaned away easily, enough for him to miss. I slid my right hand around his right wrist, just in case I needed to help him fall. Actually, he did not need much help; he was already falling on his own. My right hand gripped his wrist like a vice; his elbow was parallel to my right knee and only inches away. The rest was just polishing it up. I yanked his right arm into my knee—had to be precise on this move—needed to break it or at least dislocate his elbow to render his arm useless for now.

He screamed falling to the ground in pain holding his dangling arm. The other two punks were motionless, still sitting at their table. I walked over to them.

"Any more dancers?"

By the time I got back to my table, the two punks were dragging their buddy through the gate on their way out. The music started up again. I sat down. The butterflies had duly arrived landing in my stomach. The man at the next table collected his eyeglasses, got up and walked over to my table.

"You were marvelous, thank you!"

The accent was unmistakably Russian. He invited me to join them for dinner.

His name was Siklosy, born in Hungary forty-some years ago, but having spent the last 24 years in Moscow. Now he had been sent back to Hungary on an important assignment: to assume the personnel directorship of EXPEDITION TWO.

I never found out whether the woman companion was a romantic relation or not. Her name was Bea, and she claimed to be a distant relative of Siklosy. Real distant, I assumed.

THREE HUNDRED SIXTY...
THREE HUNDRED SIXTY-ONE...

ANDY NEVER SHOWED UP AT THE ROSE GARDEN. Probably he had gone fishing. During dinner I noticed a couple of things. First, on the left side of Siklosy's jacket just under the armpit there was a small bulge. As he moved around, I realized that he had a shoulder holster with a gun under his armpit. I wondered if things had been worse, would he have used it? Guns were issued only to KGB agents, so Siklosy had to be one. The second thing I observed that the couple seemed genuinely friendly and grateful. After long hesitation, I decided to tell Siklosy my deadly predicament even though I knew that I was taking an enormous chance. Then he told me that he knew about the purge before it was instituted. The directive came from Moscow and top Soviet officials like him were advised in advance.

He was sympathetic and offered a solution.

"Listen," he said, sounding sincere, "I owe you one. You came to help me without knowing me. You are a victim caught up in a storm at the wrong time at the wrong place and unfortunately for you, on the wrong side. If you want, I'll get you to a place where probably no one would ever think of looking for you.

"The EXPEDITION?" I asked.

"I know," he replied, "you think it's going to be some kind of hell, but it beats the gulags, if that's what you'd think is the alternative. Once this political storm is over, I'll get you out. In the meantime, you'll be on your own."

"What an irony," I thought bitterly, *"using up a favor in order to get into a labor camp."*

"And what if something happens to you, like getting transferred," I asked aloud.

"Well, that's the chance you have to take, but I'll try to warn you in advance. Besides, it won't be that hard to leave."

I took that chance only to find out that Siklosy was wrong on more than one account.

THREE HUNDRED SIXTY-SIX...
THREE HUNDRED SIXTY-SEVEN...

OW IT SEEMED TO ME AS IF THE INVISIBLE MAN AT THE BACK OF THE PLANE OPERATING THE PROJECTOR WAS SPEEDING UP THE SLIDES. He was running out of time... So was I...

***

After the incident at the Rose Garden, I returned to the small sublet apartment to say goodbye to my landlady. I packed my bag and asked her to store it for me *"til I get back."* I had a strong feeling that she knew what I meant.

"And just how long am I supposed to hang onto this suitcase, and even more importantly, how about the rental of the room?" she asked.

She was an old-timer, easily twice my age, so I used to call her "mom". Like this time.

"You know how life is, mom. Just rent the room, if I come back and you don't have a room for me, I'll just move in with you!"

She must have noticed that I said, *If* I come back, not *when*.

"I got it. If you do come back, I'll have a couch for you in the anteroom. You can try it tonight". I did, it was not comfortable at all. I never saw her or my suitcase again. I carried one change of clothing and my saved cash with me when I left early next dawn.

***

The uranium was deposited in sandstone. The mining was done on the surface, with trenches going as deep as ten feet in places. When it was necessary to go deeper, conveyor belts were installed by the Russians. At five every morning the foghorn blew and within ten minutes all units, dressed in military drab, were to line up for roll call at the front of their respective barracks. I was extremely careful about not letting anyone know that I spoke some Russian and understood even more. The less anyone knew the better off I was going to be.

Learning the golden rules of survival.

The work force was composed of two main contingents, the Russians and the Hungarians. There were about fifty Russians: the never-missing party functionaries, the tech people and security, probably KGB, and some soldiers in uniform. The Hungarian segment on the camp was composed of military units—the Hungarian People's (Red) Army. They were supposedly all recruits, but I had my doubts; some of them looked way too old to be conscripts. My assumption, that there were political "draftees" amongst them, proved to be correct.

There were some other local Hungarians employed to do all kinds of low-level work, some physical, some administrative. They were free to move around, and worked only during the day. They came in the morning, left in the evening, only to come again the next day. The "military units" were housed in barracks, where I ended up eventually. There were seven barracks, all under strict supervision; the encampment was surrounded by barbed wire in most areas.

When I showed up at the gate following the encounter with Siklosy the night before, and asked for him by name, I found that the guards already knew about me. They registered me, gave a special ID number, and thus my real name for the duration ceased to exist. I was told to find my unit. I had no idea what "my unit" was supposed to be, so I went to the Hungarian People's Army barracks, found myself what looked like an unoccupied bunk in Barrack Five and started my life in exile within the barbed wires of EXPEDITION TWO.

For days, nobody seemed to care who I was or what I was doing there. Things in the mining operation were rather loose. I assumed that Siklosy was sent from Moscow to tighten up things, including discipline, but that was yet to happen.

***

The real irony was that only four years earlier I pulled a major coup with my "Three Monkeys/Two Chairs" scenario to stay out of the Army and now I was moving in on my own.

Life can be stranger than fiction!

After less than a week of being there a uniformed man stopped me.

"Hey, who the hell are you?" he yelled. He had no bar indicating any rank on his uniform, but that did not fool me. Disguise was an integral part of Communist society more specifically of the AVO.

"I was sent here with the technical support of the Army!" I lied.

"Where is your uniform?"

"I just arrived here yesterday, got processed by the order of Comrade Siklosy. He told me not to wear a uniform!" He thought that one over. Siklosy's name, or the fact that I knew his name at all, seemed to make the necessary impression.

"Go report to Barrack Five and vanish from my sight!"

I heard him as he kept mumbling on: "Technical support, yeah… what else is coming?"

As luck would have it, I was already bunking in Barrack Five. There was no need to report; nobody cared. The next day I went to work with the rest.

Digging the trenches, I met Ivan Boros.

It was something about him that made me immediately like him; it took weeks before he began speaking of himself. He was labeled as an "imperialist agent" and was drafted into the Army. He was from the northern part of Hungary from a small city. He used to be a part-time professor at a university and also owned a small print shop that turned out to be a major problem. In the world of oppressors, possession of printing equipment alone could be a crime regardless of how archaic those presses might be. They were perceived as a potential source of publishing dissent or maybe sabotage. The system fully depended on controlling all information sources and managing the news including all printed matters. Printed information, even in small numbers outside the control of the tyrants could be deemed "threatening" to the power structure.

The pre-war Hungarian regime that supported Hitler banned Ivan from teaching his radical Marxist theories of economics and political relations. When he lost his job in academia, he moved into the printing business full time. Printing, to Ivan, became a lot more than just a job. His father was a printer and his wife's parents were in the printing business as well. He was 44 years old, but he looked twice that. He was very sick, having coughing attacks, jarring and shaking him like a leaf in a storm. When he was not coughing or digging trenches, he was smoking MUNKAS cigarettes, the worst.

Ivan joined the revolution in its early stages, actually, too early for his own good. The Social Democrats, led by Szakasits, was allowed by the Communist to exist as only a transition to the real dictatorship of the proletariat. Szakasits was later executed, but how could poor

Ivan predict that? He had printed some of the leaflets for the Social Democrats, gratis.

Around September 1952, he recalled, a truck stopped in front of his shop. Four uniformed men got off the truck and headed for the door. They were followed by a tall man in civilian clothes. He introduced himself as Gurkas, and he was rather polite as he handed over some documents. Ivan read them slowly. It was an order from the Printers Labor Union Committee, which in the Communist system was part of the ruling oligarchy; directing the removal of his printing machines.

"The Party thinks that your machines would serve the goal of Socialism a lot better if they were operated by knowledgeable comrades in the Printers Union," said Gurkas in a matter-of-fact voice, leaving no room for argument.

The uniformed men were already dismantling the presses. When they got to any complicated wiring, they reached for their wire cutters and simply cut the wires. It was obvious to Boros that they never intended to use the presses; they came ready to destroy them with wire cutters.

The vandalism broke his heart.

These presses were part of his life. Since his wife died a couple of years earlier, the presses became his only companions. He used to go down in the dead of a night just to make new adjustments, creating new and better ways to increase the efficiency of the machines and the quality of the print. As the Communists were solidifying their power, less and less printing was allotted - Ivan stayed faithfully attached to his presses anyway.

Now he begged these people not to cut the cables; he offered his help to disconnect them. Cutting those precious wires was painful for him to see but when he tried to help, they shoved him aside. For a while he tried to hang onto some of the levers he pulled so many times before, like a mother would cling to a dying child. The uniformed men finished, hauled the presses onto the truck, Gurkas followed them. At the door he stopped for a moment and turned back.

"Comrade Boros, I suggest you take my advice seriously. If anyone asks you about your damn presses, be sure to say that you donated them to the Union. Otherwise, we may remember that you were part of the Szakasits imperialist conspiracy. And that would not do you any good, would it"? Gurkas took a long look at him, then turned and left.

"Then what are you doing here?" I asked him, "Were you too stupid? Still kept talking about your presses?"

Ivan looked at me, stayed silent for a long time before he asked:

"You're not a provocateur, are you?"

I could not tell him the reason why I was there. But he did not ask me again; he did not really care. His wife dead, his presses gone, his one foot already in the grave; all he cared for were his MUNKAS cigarettes. So, he did not mind telling the rest of his saga.

"After they took my presses I no longer had a shop. People knew that I would rather give an arm than give away my presses. Anytime I said 'donated' people were trying to refrain from laughing. I took Gurkas's advice to heart, but it did not matter."

"It was summertime," Ivan continued, after another coughing attack, "and as I told you, I lived in the suburb of the city where most folks were working on the bishop's estate, others had a few acres of their own. In '49 the Communists had redistributed the bishop's estate and suddenly there were a lot of happy landowners. And because the estate was rather large, the individual pieces people got were also relatively large, between five and ten acres. It was a lot of land, especially for those who were toiling the land for someone else before."

Ivan continued: "There was a guy in the village by the name of Janos Vajda. He was a rabble-rouser, jailed under the previous Horthy regime—before the war—but somehow he escaped, and spent the years of the war underground, and surfaced after the Russians arrived. He became a local activist, pushing hard for the land reform. The hierarchy of the church, headed by the bishop, hated him. There were rumors that he was going to be excommunicated by the bishop himself, but we never knew whether it was true or not, for the bishop was shipped into labor camp and I guess his least concern was whether Vajda was still in the Holy See or not.

Janos Vajda got seven acres of prime land of the bishop's estate during the land reform. He helped to carry the chain to divvy up the land and if he had wanted, he could have gotten a piece twice as large. But that is not how Vajda's world worked. Vajda was a fair man.

Everyone was happily living in their temporary utopia until the Party decided to bring all their precious land into the kolhoz. Needless to say it was supposed to be a 'voluntary' action by the people.

That was not Vajda's world either.

He called a public meeting. Since folks in the village regarded him as their leader, a whole lot of people showed up. The gathering of the villagers was held in a packed school building and people unanimously agreed: there should not be any kolhoz in the village. Everyone went home assuming that things had been settled and that Vajda would take care of business. That was not exactly what was going to happen, not as far as the Party was concerned."

Ivan stopped talking again, gripped by another coughing attack. He was rattled uncontrollably by coughing; some greenish-looking fluid trickled out of the side of his mouth. He wiped it off with the back of his hand. I saw the bright redness of blood on his knuckles.

"Why don't you stop smoking?" I said to him halfheartedly, knowing the answer. Ivan laughed bitterly,

"Why? Smoking is the only pleasure I've got left. I won't last long anyway. They told me I have emphysema in the last stage. It's deadly. Not much time left."

I felt powerless. No words could be comforting and Ivan did not want comfort anyway. He just wanted to die without too much suffering.

"So, then how come you're here?" I asked him after his coughing subsided.

It was evening, our half-hour break between the last scoop of shoveling and dinner. Dinner was usually soup, mostly beet soup with an occasional bean here and there, and maybe sausage. A slice of a days-old loaf of bread and dark, bitter dishwater the Russians had the audacity to call "coffee."

Ivan continued his story.

"Then in '52, as I mentioned, Vajda became some kind of spokesman for the village. He was invited to meet the District Committee's Agricultural Secretary –actually he ended up meeting his assistant only since the Secretary himself was too busy with other more important issues—and Vajda was being reasoned with, politely but firmly. But Vajda, a knuckle-head, stood his ground: 'We want no kolhoz.'

'Well, we'll see,' said the Assistant Secretary at the end of the meeting.

A couple of weeks later, strange things began to happen. In the village nobody had a car. Actually not true. The doctor had an old Ford, but he packed up his family back in 1944 when the war came close, and headed west. Rumor had it that they were trapped in the Siege of Budapest and all of them got killed. All in all, after they left, nobody had a car in the village.

So it was obviously strange when one night a car, actually a truck, came out of nowhere and was slowly moving through the village. The streets were slanted toward a little hill, so you could hear the laboring of the engine of the vehicle as the truck was climbing the hills. Then you could hear when it was rolling downhill. Most of the village had stayed up, listening to the unusual sound. The truck was driving around for a couple of hours in the middle of the night then it left.

Nothing happened though for a while.

The village settled back into its normal ways, then about a week later the truck showed up again. This time it was driving around all night and left only as the sun came up. This time more jitters. Then it was peace and silence again. About a week later the true nightmare began. The truck came again and again, night after night. Every time half-dozen thugs jumped off the truck picked a house at random, no rhyme or reason. They ran up to the house, kicked the gate down, grabbed a resisting person, usually the man of the house they were after, dragged him to the truck, while the folks were screaming. They kicked the kids, the wife, old folks, if there were any, and took off. The men they took, probably gone forever. None of them had been seen since. The word was that they were in the Gulags, but who knows where?!"

Ivan took a deep breath as well and added,

"Oh yeah, Vajda. They took him during the second week. Never came back."

Even though I knew or should have known the answer, I still wanted to hear him say it, I asked again,

"Why?"

"It took us some time to figure out," said Ivan. "And yes, it was still 'us', my wife Julie was still alive. My son worked for the water department of the district. One day he came home and told us about the daily re-education they were going through: half hour indoctrination every day at the beginning of work. He —my son, Joseph—said that the Agitprop Secretary of the Party just came back from Russia, after he got his six-month training there, and had spoken about the issue of terror. He said that according to Lenin and Stalin, terror is an essential and inevitable part of the Revolution. He said it's important to create unreasonable fear to make people live in an unstable world. If you punish them, like deporting them for a reason, they understand and try to avoid creating a reason. But if you take them randomly, that would de-stabilize their world and make them live in fear. They would never know why, but the power of the State, like a sword of Damocles, would be hanging over them all the time.

The rule is: no one should feel safe!

After listening to my son, a lot of the nightmare started making sense."

Ivan started up again, "I remember," but then was interrupted by another attack; this time he was coughing up blood. He was just about to continue his story, when the whistle was blown: time for dinner.

(Ivan's story was resonating with me: very similar nightmare haunted the people of Vep, my hometown, experiencing the "trucks in the night" treatment by the Communist terror when they resisted the collectivization of the land.)

***

We had to line up three abreast and once in formation we had to start a slow run to the kitchen about a half-mile away. During the run we had to sing. A Hungarian guard, a military man in khaki with no rank showing, was the evening commander. He was a brute; someone said he was actually from Transylvania, one of those Dracula types and a brute he was. Behind his back, he was called by the soldiers, "Sergeant Gespo," someone came up with the nick name, an appropriate abbreviation of Gestapo.

Gespo was big on songs, or rather, on the singing by the soldiers while they did their marching. If the song was not sung enthusiastically enough, he yelled.

"Stop!"

The column stopped.

"We lost the song!" he yelled, "Where did we lose it"?

The drill was well known; somebody had to yell.

"We left the song under the bed, Comrade Commander!"

"Good!" He'd yell back, "Let's go back to find it!"

So now the whole column turned around and in a slow running tempo, headed back to the barracks. Everybody had to climb under the bed, looking for the song we had lost. This went on for about ten, fifteen minutes, depending on Gespo's mood of the day. Then we reassembled again. If we were running fast enough, we got to the kitchen while it was still open.

I never found out what Ivan was going to tell with the sentence that started with, "I remember…" I had to presume that his presence here in EXPEDITION TWO was because the grinding wheels of socialism finally caught up with him to penalize him for his past mistake of being on the wrong side, however minutely, of the political power struggle. Ivan's quarters were two barracks away, but the next day he did not show up at the trenches.

Apparently he was gone. I felt a huge loss. Foolishly, for a while, I hoped to see him showing up someday puffing and coughing from his MUNKAS cigarettes. I never saw him again.

***

The Russian Guard Unit at EXPEDITION TWO had three small divisions, numbering about a dozen soldiers. Each division had the responsibility to supervise one of the three enclaves of the barracks, housing about 30 or so laborers.

The unit guarding my group was commanded by Sergey.

Sergey was a huge Georgian, ostensibly from Gory, the same town from which Stalin hailed. Sergey made sure that each time he was introduced, strangers would be aware of such a lucky coincidence. Sergey had kind of a jolly personality, learned a few Hungarian words, poorly pronounced like "*te marha*" meaning you idiot ox, which was easily a fight-provoking insult amongst Hungarians, but coming off Sergey's lips it sounded funny, even condescending.

For some reason he liked me.

I had a hard time concealing my knowledge of Russian, limited as it was. Not a lot changed around the camp during the coming weeks, except the nights. It was strange because I was a good sleeper, even under stressful conditions. But after Ivan's disappearance my dreams wrapped around a dominant theme: to leave the camp, to leave the country. The final decision was probably triggered by overhearing a conversation between Sergey and a mean Chechen moron named Boris, that there were going to be some changes at the top, "Now that half-Hungarian, half-Russian Siklosy is gone."

"Whether to the Gulags or Dzerzhinsky Plaza, who knows?" Mused Sergey.

"Or maybe the Kremlin," responded Boris with a laugh, "they come and go. Some up, some down."

I got the message: nobody was going *"to let me out of here"* now that Siklosy was gone, never keeping his promise. I did not blame him; in the system it's your own hide you've got to take care of first. I came to a solid conclusion that the only way to get out of EXPEDITION TWO was by escaping. I had no idea how the "cleansing" of the system was going on the outside. I believed by now, months later, it had somewhat subsided.

Did I really need to escape or could I just walk out? I was confused. *And if getting out of here, whichever way I do, where do I go? Maybe I should just stay here in this nameless, faceless unit one of the countless grinding mills of humanity set up to serve the great socialist experiment.*

The whole country, after all, was the same as EXPEDITION TWO; it was just a larger version. An organized well-controlled concentration camp with amenities dished out to the "deserving" in the final and inevitable evolution of the Socialist Paradise, Communism.

I had some money left and some more supposedly coming from EXPEDITION TWO, but no idea how much and when. I was not about to leave a forwarding address. Other than the money issue, I had to work for the sake of work itself when I was out of here. It was a vicious cycle; if I did not work, I had no money, but it would take a longer time to be discovered. If I worked, it would take a rather short time to discover my past, and I could find myself probably in a worse place than EXPEDITION TWO. What kind of a job could I get that would not cause me to be discovered quickly? Probably low level physical labor at best. And how long would it last?

Of course, the inevitable solution kept coming back: escape from Hungary.

I had nightmares.

Recurring dreams and I always woke up in a cold sweat. In my dreams I was running through forest-covered hills, mostly uphill, chased by a dozen Russian soldiers. But I was faster. The barbed wire—it had to be the Iron Curtain, I thought—was in close proximity; I was now running parallel with it hoping for an opening. Land mines were blowing up around me, but they were blanks, big explosions with smoke puffs only. I never got hurt.

Then I saw an opening in the fence: a huge, filigreed, beautiful gate. Looking beyond the gate, I saw green hills, blue skies, little houses like they were made from candy canes, red tulips, and multicolored roses, like the ones my father used to grow in our garden. I looked back; the soldiers were gaining on me, but I was ready to roll through the gate into safety. Suddenly, the gate was blocked by a huge giant, at least ten times the size of a real person. He had a roaring laugh:

"Ha, ha, ha, we got you again! You lose!"

It was Sergey, now in real life, yelling outside the barracks to line-up for morning roll call.

I started to develop my departure plan, first from EXPEDITION TWO, making methodical plans. I checked out the fence; mostly it was barbed wire, but in some areas it was just standard fencing, altogether escapable. I started making mental notes of how and when the changing of the guards took place until I realized the problem: they were too inconsistent in their schedule I could not detect any reliable pattern. So much for meticulous planning.

Eventually my patience paid off.

One day, I overheard Sergey speaking with a couple of Russian technicians about the new exploration of the hills farther north. A bunch of Geiger counters were coming in the next day or two and there would be a small exploratory group leaving for the hills staying there for a few weeks.

Two days later, the Geiger counters were laid out next to the camp's main office. I wandered away from my unit after work, casually walking toward the large table with the counters. I passed by the guards, looked at the counters, commenting loud enough for a technician to hear.

"Wow, Geiger counters!"

The Russian tech guy walked over and asked me in broken Hungarian if I knew what the Geiger counter was for.

"Looking for gold," I replied, demonstrating a sweeping motion with my right arm.

Looked like he thought my showcasing was funny. He asked for my ID number and when the exploration team was assembled the next day, I was on it.

THREE HUNDRED SEVENTY-FIVE...
THREE HUNDRED SEVENTY-EIGHT...

THE TRIP OFFERED A GOLDEN OPPORTUNITY FOR MY "DEPARTURE". After two hours of driving north on road-less terrain, our group arrived at a previously cleared spot and set up camp. The Russians distributed the Geiger counters, explaining through an interpreter how they worked. The search was on for more uranium deposits. We were scanning the floor of a dense forest, sweeping the ground with the Geiger's angled pole and recording the numbers that showed up on the monitor. Three days later, I found myself alone. It was late in the afternoon with no one in sight. I dropped off my Geiger counter and laid my notes right next to the counter in the area where we were supposed to meet at the end of the day.

I started out north. The weather was still warm and very pleasant. I had lots of time to think, now that I had decided to leave the country.

Where am I going now? What's happening to me now? I am lost for sure but why? What did I do wrong? I tried to pursue what I wanted to be, a writer. Is that a cardinal sin against the system? Or is it much deeper: the unwillingness to comply with their decision, but who are they? What gives them the power to tell me what I want to be?

I knew that the issues were deeper than just trying to leave the country, or rather, escape the country. The issue was escaping oppression. But was it **really** oppression? Over a thousand kids at the university in Veszprem, which now seemed so far away, were studying, busy like bees buzzing in springtime. Why did they not feel oppressed? Or did they, but not telling, because they didn't want to be singled out?

"Singled out, singled out…" I was tasting the words. *Maybe that's it, being singled out…*

But who did it, was it me or was it the system? That was the big question.

I always wanted to be "me" and not one of "them".

I was a relatively good tennis player, only singles; played soccer and I was good, a good goalie, that is. Seldom did I join any group; then when I had to, I never felt comfortable.

"Gee, that must have been it!" I singled myself out! Appointed myself a general, a general without armies. I recalled what Manny said at the university: the Party does not need generals the Party needs soldiers, like those at Stalingrad, all one million of them. All one million of them all right…dead! I guess I was not born to be a soldier," I concluded. I also realized that nobody was born to be a general, either. Hitler was painting Austrian apartments for a living; Stalin was holding up payroll trucks before he came to rule the world, or at least half of it. *What does it take? What am I missing?* These were the critical pieces of the puzzle. Then of course all those haunting questions, those self-doubts, translated into a search for a solution.

I am leaving the country.

But the doubts were still there. Was it because the system rejected me with my occasional, half-hearted overtures, or did I reject the system where soldiering was a way of life, the only way of life? The country was halved in two, one segment for obedient citizen-soldiers, who like ants, were trained, groomed, programmed by the Party, like my schoolmates; the other one for nameless, faceless, useless pariahs. Branded and treated as rebels. Like me. The tragedy of the lonely animal, separated from the herd. Destined to starve, while the rest were heading to the slaughterhouse happily because they've been fed. Fattened for the slaughter.

The system was ruthless.

No room for mistakes. No room for forgiveness. One did not have to make a mistake. What was absolutely right today could become an unforgivable wrong tomorrow. Some invisible Goliath somewhere, too high up to be touched, made decisions of what is black and what's white, and dished out rewards or penalties accordingly.

Who were those invisible Goliaths? And how come, at some point, they would fall too?

Because fall they did. In the late 30's in Russia, Stalin, in his paranoia, executed thirty or so of his forty-five generals. A few of them in person just to be sure. At the end, as rumors had it, he was most likely poisoned by his "faithful comrade" right in the Politburo.

So, who was safe in the system?

No one.

Escape. It seems to be the only answer. Or is it?

What kind of a pie-in-the-sky dream was that? There was no escape from this land, you were condemned to live and die here. Nobody knew the real statistics, except that since the Iron Curtain was built, escaping had become virtually impossible. The Communists built the Iron Curtain to "keep the agents of Imperialism out" while in fact it was really opened only to them and for their precious currency. The border was supposedly escape proof.

A passenger's ID was checked by AVH Border Patrol on every train heading west from Budapest, which was about a hundred miles from the border. Trains were the primary way to travel. Fifteen miles from the border a passenger had to provide proof of residence or a reason for traveling, or show a special travel permit. About one mile from the actual border, the forests or meadows were wired with a network of a hidden alarm system. Once any part of the wire was tripped, a flare shot to the sky, visible for miles; this was an alarm to the AVH. Then there was the "Snake", the actual border, the Iron Curtain. First, a ten-foot wide strip of land on the Hungarian side of the barbed wire fence freshly plowed and raked daily. It was designed to show even the footsteps of a rabbit running across, ensuring that the AVH unit in charge of that particular segment of the border could be held accountable for escapes. A 100 mile long border separating Hungary from Austria was divided into a thousand foot-long segments guarded by over 300 machine gun towers. Each section was under the supervision of an AVH unit, including manning the machine guns. A footstep in your section, comrade, and you had better produce the perpetrator, dead or alive; otherwise heads would roll. There were two sets of barbed wires, each six feet tall, running parallel about six feet apart. In between was the minefield, interconnected with tripwires. Most of them were covered by foliage, some already tripped by wild animals.

Deer, rabbits, mountain lions…

The border wound around like a giant snake. Sometimes, it created a huge deceptive, an almost 360 degree loop. There was a story going around about a small group of escapees who developed an ingenious plan: they carried a 25 feet long ladder and somehow managed to carry all the way to border undetected. They laid the ladder across the barbed wires and one by one they climbed across above the minefield to Austria. As they were running happily, a few hundred feet later they encountered another set of double-barbed wire similar to the one they had just crossed. They were puzzled first then came to a conclusion that the Austrians built their own borders as well, so after some hesitation they climbed again. It was one of those tight loops of the border. It was late night, and the poor idiots were back into the welcoming arms of the AVH.

I had no idea how I was going to escape, but I was convinced that when the noose tightened a bit more, in the do-or-die stage, I would figure it out.

But what about afterwards?

Let's assume I succeeded with the escape and ended up, like everybody else, in an Austrian refugee detention camp. There were horror stories about those camps, like three or more years in detention before immigrating.

Immigrate to where?

Austria did not care for Hungarian refugees. The Soviet occupation barely ended in 1954; the Austrians were still scared of the Russians. The common fear was that they might come back to reoccupy the country any minute. And they, the Russians, would not look with favor upon Austria harboring fleeing Hungarians, now would they?!

How about France?

They used to accept Hungarians, mostly for cannon fodder for their Southeast Asian venture. Since the Bien Dien Phu debacle in Vietnam, they were not taking Hungarians for their famous Foreign Legion either. That organization had long since disintegrated.

West Germany, occupied by the Americans, was a country almost impossible to enter into. That left Canada, Australia, and the USA. Three years in an Austrian refugee camp, then if lucky, immigrate to the USA.

What about the USA?

Was it the "land of opportunity" as dreamed by the millions of pariahs of the world? Or was it just another collectivist system with more monies to spread around? *How will I ever fit into any system even if I successfully escape against all odds? Are places there for generals, or is it still soldiering in a fancier uniform? What could I offer? I don't even have my engineering degree, or any degree. What is my literary talent, if I have any at all? And what's more, what will I do in a land whose language is strange to me?*

Then what about the consequences for those I leave behind?

My dad, my mom, not only the pain that I'll cause by never seeing them again, but the repercussions! I knew about those as did everybody else. The Communists made sure that the relatives of the few lucky ones who made it out, or even those who just tried, would pay the price.

Then why?

What is "there" on the other side of the Iron Curtain, beyond the Austrian refugee camps, beyond the pain and sufferings? What is "there" that makes it worth all the sacrifices?

The magic word was FREEDOM.

The elusive dream sought by mankind for millennia.

They say they have it in America.

But who are "they"? Some distant relatives of folks in a village somewhere, who immigrated decades ago, in better, more peaceful times, and ostensibly made a fortune at least by the village's standards? How many were like that? One out of ten? One out of a hundred? One out of a thousand? How about those who never made it "big"? Were they what the Commies claimed them to be: the exploited downtrodden slaves of imperialism?

What is the truth?

Probably the most powerful and believable evidence came from the Communists themselves. There was this generally accepted, albeit ironic, rule to consider: whatever the Party said about anything that they had no proof to either verify or deny, you simply had to take the exact opposite view of what the Party said, and you were as close to the truth as you'd ever get without actual proof. Using this reliable standard of evaluation, I concluded that America must be the place to go.

My first goal was to get to Lake Balaton, less than a hundred miles away to start my new life. I've heard at EXPEDITION TWO that in Siofok, the largest resort city on the shores of Lake Balaton, there was a major construction project under way. Maybe there is a laborer's job for me.

In real life I had a small issue to deal with: transportation. I was limited to my two feet—they for walking—and to one arm, that's for waving at passing camions trying to get a lift. About half way between EXPEDITION TWO and Lake Balaton there was a small city called Szekszard. One of my few close friends at the university was Leon, hailing from Szekszard. I even visited him at his parents' home a couple of years back which now seemed more like eons. Leon's parents had a small winery, a few acres, but with their devoted work, care and commitment to excellence, they were able to provide a decent life for their family. That of course was before the Communists took over. Now the winery was no longer theirs but they were allowed to work there, mostly because nobody else had the expertise of being a wine-maker. I had high hopes to find them.

The first night I spent near a farmhouse. Huge hay bales on the ground afforded me a great sleep. What a great sleep it was! Bright sparkling stars the wonderful scent of freshly harvested hay, no Sergey, no roll calls, no trenches. The next afternoon, after catching a couple of short rides and adding a few miles of straight walk, I found Leon's parents' cottage in Szekszard, before sunset. They were extremely kind people, never asked questions. Not what was I doing there, not where am I going, where I was coming from. We lived in a world where the less you knew about others the less danger you faced.

"Don't worry about paying the money back" was their only comment as they offered to loan me some money that I badly needed and reluctantly accepted.

They invited me to stay for dinner with them. A real dinner! There was an extra bunk bed in the vinery; I was invited to stay overnight. The next morning I was up before sunrise and left. Three lucky hitchhikes and the third day of my exodus I arrived in the city of Siofok.

THREE HUNDRED SEVENTY-NINE...
THREE HUNDRED EIGHTY...

BECAME A VAGRANT LABORER. I knew that even as such, I should not stay at any job too long. I moved from job to job. Anais and I got married in a clandestine, non-ceremonial event in Szombathely in September 1955. The judge who performed the official act was a personal acquaintance of my biological mother, Roza. She used to work for the judge's family, washing and ironing into the wee hours of the morning in better times. During the fall I worked on a construction site around Lake Balaton, mostly carrying steel rods for a new building. Then in late October I moved closer to Budapest, since every weekend I was taking the train to Ujfeherto, to see Anais. Those weekends were the only things in my life that mattered.

Actually, I did not live in Budapest because I could not. In order to reside in Budapest one had to have a residency permit stamped into one's ID book, and unless the person was either born in Budapest, or lived

185

there prior to the Communists, those permits were hard to come by. Budapest was the only city where foreigners had contact with Hungary, and the Communists were careful to maintain their image.

I lived on the outskirts of Budapest in barracks-type labor housing at Kobanya in the heart of proletariat land. Eight of us lived in a relatively small room that had four bunk beds. We worked different shifts, so two of us had to share the same bed, alternating. In late November I worked in a brick factory, pushing clay-filled wheelbarrows from the area where trucks unloaded the clay for the furnaces.

That year winter came early and hard. By the middle of December, I could no longer bear the bone-chilling cold and asked the union representative to transfer me to work at the furnaces, at least for a while.

"I'll see what I can do. I'll look up your file in personnel," he promised. That was my last day at the brick factory; I had to move on, keeping a step head of information regarding my background called "Kader."

For the next three weeks, I worked at the produce market, unloading what seemed to be millions of tons of potatoes, cabbages, sugar beets and fruits. It wasn't long before I got caught eating an apple on the job; the supervisor saw it and I was fired. After the first of the year I got what seemed to be a real winner, a job at an optical factory called MOM. The word was the acronym for Hungarian Optical Works on the Buda side of the Danube. I was hired to work on the prescription glass manufacturing assembly line.

"*Great!*" I enthused. "*Working on the assembly line in a warm building!*" But the place turned out to be, if not hell, at least a purgatory! The temperature in the assembly line building was over 110 F. Dozens of workers, like myself, were standing next to conveyor belts, half-naked, sweating. I was working on the lens-grinding line and the work was absolutely cruel. Cast iron modules, about the size of a basketball cut in half, hollow with eight circular indentations on the inner walls where the lenses to be ground were fit. The iron cast half-basketball was first heated up in a furnace then the inside walls were covered with boiling tar. The job called for dropping the yet to be ground lenses into those indentations, now covered with boiling tar, and make them fit snug. Then the whole unit was cooled off, the lenses were seated frozen in their indentation, solidly. The steel basketball was sent to the grinding assembly, ground to the required angle, and then the lenses had to be taken out of the indentations. The same procedure was repeated; the metal basketballs were heated up, and the folks at the assembly line picked the lenses out with their fingertips real fast.

I worked on the segment of the conveyor belt where the lenses were taken out. In February, I moved to Labatlan, the village that was home to the largest cement factory in Hungary twenty miles west of Budapest, on the southern bank of the Danube.

I got a job and met George.

THREE HUNDRED EIGHTY-FIVE...
THREE HUNDRED EIGHTY-SIX...

EORGE USED TO BE A HUNGARIAN AIR FORCE TEST PILOT, ONE OF THEIR YOUNGEST AND BRIGHTEST. As the Communists took control of the Armed Forces it became mandatory for an officer to be a member of the Party as well. George, a lieutenant at the time, loved to fly, but he was not willing to pay the price the Communists wanted to charge: membership in the Party. First he was demoted to mechanical duties, then to ground crew. When the Air Force finally ditched him, he ended up in Labatlan, driving a dump truck, hauling clay to the kilns where I worked.

George was also a boxer, fighting on the factory's boxing team.

One night after our shift, he invited me to the gym for a workout.

The team was preparing for an all-important match against an old rival, Tata. I got into the ring for a couple of rounds of sparring. The director of factory sports activities was among those watching.

A week later, I got an offer from the Labor Union Secretary to coach the boxing team. The temptation was too strong to resist, it had too many built-in goodies: a much better job, and maybe a factory apartment. Anais could come to join me; we'd live as husband and wife. I was too anxious to make life happen, I forgot the ground rule: the Party won't forget and won't forgive.

I made the obvious mistake. I accepted the job. In early March, the Party arranged for us to move into a small, government apartment near the factory.

Anais arrived a week later.

Our team was winning; the power structure was proud of the team's accomplishment—athletics meant a lot to the Party. My star was rising.

Instinctively, I knew that my rising star, as always, would be my downfall.

The Party's secretary called me to his office one day in early June. He wanted to discuss my "past activities" that had just recently come to his attention. Knowing what my fate would be once he found out about my past, I played the only card I could.

"It will have to wait a couple of weeks, at least. I am heavily involved in training for very important matches coming up" I told him, trying to hide my concern.

To my surprise he agreed, with some reluctance.

The road map of my life seemed to constantly repeat itself. After a while I would end up at the inevitable crossroads, with no good way out.

It must be different this time. I got tired of running.

There was a boxer on our team, Bolla, the heavyweight, a mediocre amateur and a great guy. He was George's truck driving partner; and because of their time spent together he knew of George's background as a pilot.

You can plan your life down to the very minute details as long as you understand that there is a Divine power that usually has no regards for your planning. The two pieces of news—one that my questionable past is about to catch up with me again and that George is an ex-pilot—came out of nowhere, almost simultaneously; although the first one was bound to happen any day.

But to find an ex Air Force pilot not only at the place I worked but on my boxing team? If that is not the answer to my prayers...

But is it?

Who is he?

In Hungary, under the Communists, fortunes could change with extreme speed and my life was a sad testimony attesting to that fact.

But what about George's life? Why was he out of the service? Did they let him go from a precious position of flying military planes, probably even jets, allowing him to go on the loose?

How would I approach him with my plans that are vague at best, although they were beginning to take shape rapidly: if you can't cross the Iron Curtain on the ground, what about trying to cross it in an airplane? Nobody in history had ever tried to cross it this way! To me, this could mean only one of two things: that it simply *could not be done*, that escaping by air was impossible. Or, perhaps, it really meant something else - that there had never been anyone *with the skills to do it*, at least not until now. In truth, my "plan" was not much of a "plan" at all—I had no idea as to the "what" or "how" to do it, but George being a pilot meant that if in my yet to be devised plan, my dream of crossing the Iron Curtain meant escaping by air, then he could be the one element that could make it happen.

But how am I going to approach him? I don't know anything about him, except that he certainly does not belong in this place. Would he join an escape plan if we could create one? What about the idea of escaping? If he ever wanted to escape he had nothing but wide open opportunities, for time and again he was sitting in the cockpit of a warplane and, if he chose to, thirty minutes later regardless at what part of Hungary he was flying, he would be on the other side of the Iron Curtain. And in case he were to fly one of the latest Russian MIG jets and would have landed in the West he could become famous, even rich. So the likelihood of him having any interest to escape is low, if not remote.

On the other hand, I had no choice. I must either approach him or miss perhaps my only opportunity for freedom, even if approaching him meant exposing me once and for all.

If he is either a planted informer of the regime, or if he just wanted to make points to get back to the Air Force by turning me in, that would be the risk I would have to take.

Do I want to be such a naked target?

Should I try to feel him out without exposing myself? Or just wait and see if maybe he'll approach me if I send some signal? But why would he come to me, I have nothing to offer as a contribution to an escape plan that is not even hatched? It's him, or rather his skills, that I knew to be essential.

The days became restless and the nights were filled with tortures of the soul. How am I going to tell Anais? Is she going to come along? She has no reason to escape other than being my wife. But should I even ask her? What are the chances of success whatever the escape would be? What would the consequences be if we fail? For me it would probably be death by hanging. For her it would be most likely the same.

As the days passed, however, my mind started to find strength and clarity. The importance of the escape overwhelmed everything else. I made the decision: I could take my raw desire for freedom and draw on it to forge an unbending will to escape, and I could trust that this will would be strong enough to convince George to come aboard my escape plan. Once I made a final decision to approach George, my mind became clear and unchangeable.

The rest was just dealing with the details.

The time had come: it was now or never for my long dormant plans.

After a Wednesday training session, I invited George for a drink at a beer bar next to the factory's grocery shop. After the first round of beers I opened up.

"George, I have to get out of Hungary!"

George took a swig from his beer mug his eyes were half-closed as he swallowed seemingly in sheer joy. Then he put his mug down.

"What about your proud boxing team?!"

George had a way to put sarcasm in his voice without extra effort. Then he took another swig before he got to the subject at hand.

"It is impossible!"

I would not let it go.

"George, there IS a way."

"Oh?"

I sensed his interest rising, the door was beginning to open. Time came to turn on the power:

"Oh, yes! There is. If we can't cross the barbed wire by walking through we can always fly across high above. More precisely: you can."

"You've got a loose airplane hanging around that I should know about?"

"No, I don't, but MALEV has!" I said. MALEV was the Hungarian Airline owned by the government.

It was late afternoon. The sun was still above the horizon. We were sitting at the outdoor area of a beer joint. Suddenly, as if directed by some invisible force we both looked up. Way up north a white condensation streak was crayoned on the blue velvet sky, probably drawn by the exhaust of a military aircraft. I looked across the table above the beer mugs, straight into George's eyes and slowly, but very clearly, pronounced the words,

"George, for us there is no hope in this forlorn country. Life only gets more hopeless every day. You have nowhere to go, and for me it's worse: I am at the end of my rope. That sign up there is like prophecy and you were given heaven's approval. More than approval: an assignment by God!"

George's hand was halfway toward his face, raising his mug, but the move never got finished. His hand stopped in midair, then he put the mug down and reached for my hand.

"I guess we just got a mission for us, didn't we?"

I knew that the handshake meant an irrevocable commitment.

For life or death.

THREE HUNDRED NINETY... THREE HUNDRED NINETY-ONE...

NOW THE SLIDES WERE CLICKING WITH FEROCIOUS SPEED. My palms began to sweat as I reached into my bag and grabbed the handle of the pipe wrench.

Oh God! Stop the clock now! Stop EVERYTHING! The time, the Earth, the plane, E-V-E-R-Y-T-H-I-N-G!

The slides continued clicking with no mercy.

Two weeks after the first meeting with George, I decided to break the news to Anais. It took me all that two weeks, weighing the potential, deadly consequences of bringing her along, compared to those of leaving her behind and never to see her again.

She took it calmly, matter-of-factly.

"*When?*" she asked.

It was still June and the date was yet to be set.

195

In order to make sure that I couldn't change my mind, I had to burn all our bridges. Around late June, we packed one small suitcase and a sports bag and disappeared from Labatlan without a word, without a trace. We hoped.

So much for the appointment to "review my past political activities" with a moron party hatchet man...

THREE HUNDRED NINETY-SEVEN...

THE NEXT TWO WEEKS WERE PURE HELL WITH ENDLESS PARANOIA. We were hanging out at the strangest places, mostly around Budapest. Since Charlie's parents were on vacation; we spent a few days there, making sure that the "block observer" usually a Party apparatchik, did not notice our presence. Then we stayed at Gabor's place briefly: he was a university student in Budapest, had a permit for legitimate residency. I had a distant cousin and her husband they lived in the outskirts of Budapest, on the Buda side in the mountains we stayed with them 'til we wore the guest staying-time too thin.

I was becoming paranoid at times. Anais was handling the pressure more evenly. On July 8th, Sunday, the entire team met at a regional park on the Buda side. Charlie brought some good news. A friend of his, he said, was assistant manager of a small hotel in Buda, near Margit Bridge. The head manager went for a weeklong vacation, and Charlie's friend was left in charge. We could move into the hotel with some amount of safety. No registration, no names just referencing the room number.

"That's great" I said, "because we don't need the place for a whole week anyway!"

A monumental silence.

Suddenly everyone realized that a so far undecided date had been set, and we now had entered the road of no return.

"I've made arrangements to get airline tickets. We are going to an exhibition boxing match in Szombathely. It's HA-LIG Flight 387, next Friday."

Silence was looming, 'til Charlie broke it.

"Hell guys, that's Friday the Thirteenth!"

"Yes, Charlie," said George "it sure is" and everybody knew that it was an unchangeable affirmation.

THREE HUNDRED NINETY-EIGHT...

WE MOVED INTO THE SMALL HOTEL. It was peaceful and quiet. The agreement was not to use the phone, there was only one in the lobby anyway, and not to use our names unless confronted by authorities.

My paranoia subsided somewhat. The imaginary predators went away.

Until Tuesday night...

THREE HUNDRED NINETY-NINE...

HE PROJECTOR STOPPED: IT MUST HAVE RUN OUT OF SLIDES.
The slide show was over.
The real show was just beginning.

CHAPTER X

10,000 Feet in Szil airspace, Hungary
Friday, July 13, 1956 1440 Hour

THE DC-3 WAS HUMMING AT TEN THOUSAND FEET. My breath became shorter, shallower. I tried to call on my martial arts training to override the autonomous controls of my breathing, but it did not work. Panic began to show its ugly face, fear was its engine. It was running at full throttle.

"I need to get to George and tell him to abort," I murmured to myself.

Then the sheer thought of aborting panicked me even more. I felt that I was transported away from the plane somewhere into a sun parched wheat field. I could see myself swinging my scythe, rhythmically, slowly. I could see my mother smiling at me when I turned around, as she was folding the wheat into neat bundles as they were peacefully falling to the ground, slowly filling up the field.

So, so peacefully until the image vanished.

Abort... abort... abort, my brain was screaming but the words evaporated before they could reach my mouth, melting around my lips to form salty saliva. I was wiping my mouth with the back of my hand. Time seemed to come to a complete standstill.

The running of the propellers of the DC-3 became a soft rhythmic drumbeat, the drumbeat of a familiar song, although I could not quite figure out why the song sounded so familiar. Then the summer image came back again, the cabin was transformed into a gently rolling wheat field soaked by an enormous amount of sunshine, the like of it I had never seen. Somewhere in the corner of my mind, though, I vaguely remembered that I actually was on an airplane, but I thought it may have already landed and I should now be ready to deplane.

The sound of the propellers changed from a soft drumbeat into the ear-splitting sounds of a ticking clock. TICK-TOCK, TICK-TOCK, TICK-TOCK.

"What was my count?" The last I remembered, it was three hundred and ninety five. Maybe ninety nine... Maybe it has long passed four hundred. Maybe George heard me and aborted the takeover fight and...

Now George stood up and my scattered thoughts vanished. My brain zapped back into reality: The final count.

THE FREE FOR ALL

FOUR HUNDRED...

EORGE WAS SITTING AT THE BULKHEAD NEXT TO THE COCKPIT DOOR ON THE STARBOARD SIDE OF THE PLANE, FACING THE PASSENGER CABIN.

He looked very casual when he got up. He was holding my book in his left hand. Then he looked around, opened the book with his right hand, removed the gun, closed the book, and handed it over to a balding passenger, sitting across the aisle.

"Sholokhov. Great reading, do you mind holding it?"

The man looked up at George, like being in a hypnotic trance, he reached for the book. For a second the scene reminded me of a religious ritual. Then George's gun came down on the balding head butt first, about two inches above the temple, right at the receding hairline.

For a second nothing seemed to be happening. The entire universe froze. Then George brought the gun down for the second time. The man slumped forward, dropped the book. Blood was beginning to drip from his forehead. The world, that a moment ago was at a standstill, now started spinning.

I grabbed the passenger sitting in front of me with my left hand. I was convinced that this one was the AVO agent. The pipe wrench was in my right hand. The man's eyes were wide open; I saw a lake full of alligators, the animals of death. I realized that if I brought the pipe wrench down on his head it would probably kill him.

No killing! The instinctive thought flashed through my brain. I dropped the pipe wrench and hit him with my fist. His eyes closed, the alligators were gone. The man collapsed into his seat without moving. Charlie, obsessed with his billy club, kept hitting the same passenger over and over again.

"Charlie! Stop it!" screamed Anais standing straight up from her chair. I was wondering why.

Charlie turned around "Sorry" he said evenly with no real regret as he turned on his heels and brought down his billy club on the next passenger.

All in all the fight was not going well.

The seating arrangement, which was essential to our success, was screwed up in the first place, and now confusion took over. Our plan of disarming everyone within three seconds was long gone. A couple of passengers far from being "neutralized" were beginning desperately to defend themselves. By now everyone in the passenger cabin seemed to be on their feet, fighting or falling and screaming. The cabin became so loud that I could hardly hear the roar of the engines. I was already searching passengers for the gun.

Where the hell is the AVO man?

George still stood at the front of the passenger cabin holding the Zbrojovka in a sweeping motion, his eyes searching for the fatal move to come from the disguised AVO agent.

He's got to be here.

Was he still conscious or had he been already knocked out?

If he was still conscious, then George and the two rusty bullets were our only hope. It seemed that we were already more than a minute into the fight: three of seven passengers were knocked out. Charlie and Bolla were on their feet as we were all frantically searching for the elusive but all important gun. Still facing the passenger cabin, George made one step forward away from the cockpit door. He was sweeping his gun slowly from side to side.

I looked up. The cockpit door cracked slightly ajar.

"George! The door!" I yelled at the top of my voice.

George spun around, but it was too late.

The cockpit door, which opened slightly just as I looked up, now was slammed. A second later the DC-3 dropped its nose at a steep angle and began to accelerate downward.

All hell broke loose in the cabin.

CHAPTER XI

Somewhere between Five Hundred and Ten Thousand feet over Hungary.

THE PLANE WAS NOW ALL OVER THE SKY LIKE A PING PONG BALL IN A WIND TUNNEL. When the crew realized the attack, they began to execute emergency procedures designed for the "unlikely event" of an armed takeover attempt. They dropped the nose of the DC-3, brought the aircraft into a steep dive. Heavy G forces came into play. After a dive of a thousand feet or so they leveled off the plane briefly, and then brought her into a virtual stall before a sharp climb.

To be followed by another nose-dive.

While the G forces were tearing the interior of the passenger cabin apart, fatal structural damage to the aircraft was not likely. One thing was certain; no one would be able to remain on their feet in the passenger cabin. No one did. The unsecured wooden crates were sliding back and forth like roller coasters down the aisle, crashing everything in their path. Sandwiched between the sliding luggage, rollicking crates, anyone unlucky enough to be in their destructive path was knocked out.

The panels of the corrugated aluminum floor came loose. As the plane went into a stall, the entire mass of boxes, panels of the floor, and passengers floated to the ceiling. I was tossed around like a leaf in a thunderstorm. In one moment I was knocked against the floor, in the next I was glued to the ceiling, all in defiance of gravity.

I was floating near the roof of the cabin when I felt a ripping draft.

My eyes were searching for Anais. I spotted her. She seemed to be unconscious, a few feet from me rolling on the floor toward the front of the plane. Her clothes were ripped and her face was bleeding.

The plane was climbing again.

The loose contents of the cabin were sliding backwards now. As she slid past me, I was able to grab her ankle with my right hand. With my left hand I was hanging on to the frame of the nearest, now empty, seat. It was bolted to the floor. Powerful forces were tearing at me as I was holding desperately to the frame of the seat. Then my hand lost its grip, I was breaking away. Less than ten feet away from me, the door of the DC-3 was now cracked open. I could hear it flopping against the doorframe of the fuselage.

A frightening thought flashed into my brain: *we'll be sucked out.* *Oh God, no, no!*

He must've heard me, for He sent us the first break. The plane rolled into another nose-dive, in the last moment and the entire contents of the passenger cabin including myself and Anais plummeted forward.

*** *

Up front George was holding on tight. Being closer to the front of the plane, the violent forces were somewhat minimized where he stood. Moments earlier Bolla managed to toss a screwdriver to George, he caught it in mid-air with one hand. An amazing cool juggler's act! Then he went to work on the door.

Another break.

Subsequent investigation established that of the six DC-3s flown domestic routes by MALEV, HA-LIG Flight 387 was the only one with a plywood cockpit door. The other five aircrafts of the commercial fleet had already been equipped with aluminum doors. The plywood was ripping apart fast under the pressure of George's screwdriver. Once the hole cracked in the plywood was large enough, George forced apart the latch locking the door and busted the cockpit door open. He expected to face four crewmembers: pilot, co-pilot, maybe an engineer, perhaps a radioman at the most.

He was wrong. There were five.

CHAPTER XII

Inside HA-LIG Flight 387, Over Hungary
Friday, July 13, 1956 at 1445 Hour

ELEK DOKTOR WAS A POLICE LIEUTENANT IN THE EMPLOY OF THE HUNGARIAN AVO. The last two years he'd been assigned to air security. The job was a piece of cake. To fly with HA-LIG Flight 387, he had to be at Ferihegy airport by noon. The flight took about fifty minutes to Szombathely, then after a short hop on to Zalaegerszeg, the final destination, another 20 minutes. Then back to Budapest. He would be home by six o'clock in the evening. In addition to having an easy job, Elek Doktor was fascinated by airplanes.

When he had come of age, he did his four years in the Army. He liked the service. Then he was recruited by the AVO, after two years of special training, he was assigned to "airline security." His brother was already a captain in the AVO, which helped maintaining his position.

The flights were uneventful.

He loved to sit in the cockpit, chatting with the crew. Even though it was tight quarters, he felt very comfortable there. The ritualistic procedures of the take-off and landing fascinated him along with the sophisticated instrumentation of the plane. The regular crew liked him too. Of course, he knew that he was not supposed to be in the cockpit during the flight, but as long as the crew did not mind it, what's the difference?

When he first heard the commotion in the passenger cabin on this Friday, he thought someone must've gotten sick. He put on his jacket, buttoned up his gun holster; and then pushed his gun, a Walther PPK snug into its leather holder. The noise from the passenger cabin alerted the rest of the crew as well. As Doktor stepped toward the door, the mechanic squeezed himself between him and the door.

"Cover me, I'll check it out!" said the mechanic when he opened the door and peeked out.

"Jesus!" he yelled the forbidden word and jerked the door shut.

"People with weapons!" Then he screamed at the pilot.

"Dive! Dive hard!!"

Captain Saros assumed full command.

"Call MAYDAY! Call in emergency landing," he ordered the radioman.

"Prepare for emergency landing! Procedures!"

"Shoot through the door! Shoot now!" yelled the mechanic at Doktor.

"Relax. They'll be stopped," Doktor said calmly referring to the attackers on the other side of the locked cockpit door. He removed his PPK out of its holster, pulled back the top of the mechanism then released it. The sliding top slid forward, picked up the first bullet from the magazine and delivered it into the chamber.

Now the PPK was loaded, ready for action and so was AVO Lieutenant Elek Doktor.

CHAPTER XIII

Soviet Airbase near Papa, Hungary
Friday, July 13, 1956 at 1445 Hour

L IEUTENANT KUBILEVSKY, A SOVIET AIR FORCE OFFICER, WAS ASSIGNED TO RADAR DUTIES EACH DAY BETWEEN EIGHT IN THE MORNING AND SOMETIME AROUND THREE IN THE AFTERNOON AT THE PAPA AIRBASE.

It was an easy shift.

Life was rather routine, actually boring, at the base during the summer of 1956, with a Soviet Air Defense Fighter Unit occupying the farthest western Soviet air base in Hungary. It was less than a hundred miles east of the Austrian-Hungarian border. Three wings of three MIG-17s each; the pride of the Soviet Air Force, commissioned four years earlier, replaced the vintage MIG 15's at the base. Practice flights were executed twice a day, thirty minutes in the morning and thirty minutes at sundown. Radar facilities at the airbase monitored two commercial flights; one from Budapest to Szombathely which then continued on to

Zalaegerszeg, another Hungarian city, and the return of the same flight to Budapest later in the day.

They were the slow-flying DC-3s (Li-2) of MALEV.

He usually picked up the flight as it left the airspace of Szil. This day was no different. HA-LIG reported in giving altitude and coordinates, albeit a few minutes later than usual, then signed off.

Five minutes later came a totally unexpected call.

"MAYDAY! MAYDAY! HA-LIG Flight 387. We are attempting an emergency landing!"

He was responding:

"Flight 387 Come in! Flight 387 Come in!"

There was no answer.

Lieutenant Kubilevsky picked up the phone and dialed the base commander.

***

Colonel Probishenko, commander of the Soviet airbase at Papa was having lunch outside of his office in a small, shady garden, just a few yards from his desk. It was a hot day. He and Captain Bazilevskaya were in a yard where the light breeze brought some relief from the heat of the scorching July sun.

They finished lunch. When the phone rang, he asked the captain to answer it.

Bazilevskaya walked into the colonel's office, picked up the phone, listened for a few seconds then called over to Probishenko:

"I think you better take this one!"

The colonel got up, annoyed by the interruption.

"What is it?"

The news from Lieutenant Kubilevsky did not disturb the colonel at all.

It was not possible for the DC-3 to just vanish into thin air.

"Listen Kubilevsky, planes just don't disappear. I suggest that you get back to your radar screen and pay a bit closer attention and report to me as soon as you hear from that 'gooney bird'." Then he hung up.

"He is sure goofy at times," he said to Bazilevskaya, who was standing next to him during the phone conversation. He went back to the porch and continued on with his reading.

The colonel was dead wrong, but he would not know it for another five minutes.

CHAPTER XIV

Soviet Airbase Papa, Hungary
Friday, July 13, 1956 at 1450 Hour

 OLONEL PROBISHENKO'S PHONE RANG AGAIN. When he picked up the phone, he had a good idea where the call came from.

"Lieutenant?"

"Yes Colonel!"

"Where is HA-LIG?"

"Disappeared colonel!"

"Any contact since MAYDAY?"

"No Colonel, none"

Probishenko clicked the phone down and turned to Basilevskaya,

"Call Comrade Andropov on the secure line!"

Comrade Yuri Andropov was the highest-ranking Soviet authority over both civilian and military forces stationed in Hungary. Even though his title was ambassador, he was THE ultimate boss.

It took some time even though the call was put through emergency lines to Andropov. Operational directive was requested as to whether the fighters should pursue the DC-3 regardless of whether it was under the control of the regular crew or of hostile forces; should it be forced or shot down, and most importantly, should the fighters enter into Austrian airspace to follow Flight 387.

According to available records, Andropov, while agreeing to all actions requested, denied permission for the fighters to penetrate Austrian airspace, perhaps fearing an international outcry. Austria was a neutral nation, its neutrality guaranteed by the Soviets less than two years earlier. Apparently, the decision was to pursue HA-LIG flight 387, unless it had crashed already or would crash before the MIGs could catch up with it and force it to land while still in Hungarian airspace.

The three MIG 17s of Wing 2, under the command of Captain Bazilevskaya, were air-born within minutes, even before the conversation between Probishenko and Andropov finished, roared off the runway heading west.

(The specific details of the events at the airbase were narrated by Laszlo four months later, see Epilogue.)

CHAPTER XV

*The Cockpit of Flight 387 at 10,000 Feet over Hungary
Friday, July 13, 1956 at 1455 Hour*

THE SON OF A BITCH WAS IN THE COCKPIT ALL ALONG THOUGHT GEORGE, AS HE FACED THE FIFTH MAN AND STARED INTO THE BARREL OF ELEK DOKTOR'S WALTHER PPK. The AVO agent was waiting for George fully prepared, while trying to steady himself on the bouncing plane, with his gun in hand.

George aimed the Zbrojovka with two bullets, one in the chamber and one in the magazine, slightly above the head of the AVO man and pulled the trigger.

There was a small click.

Ten-year old bullets just don't work that well, he thought, as he smashed the useless gun onto the forehead of Elek Doktor with full force.

The plane rolled into another nose-dive throwing the already dazed AVO agent straight up to the ceiling with his feet off the floor dangling in the air. He was hanging on to some protruding gadgets from the cockpit's roof with his left hand, holding his gun in his right. Then for an infinitely small time, his memory deserted him. He could not remember whether he loaded his Walther PPK or not. When the plane went into a sharp climb he got slammed to the floor and had a chance to act. His years of training took over: when in doubt, reload. Elek Doktor, pulled the top of his gun back released it again, aimed at George's chest and pulled the trigger.

It was then that Doktor realized that he made a deadly mistake. The gun was loaded already before he tried to reload it. Trying to load it for the second time, the ejector failed to catch the perimeter of the first bullet already in the chamber, an unlikely, rare event. The top of the gun slid forward regardless, picked up the second bullet from the magazine and that second bullet got stuck halfway between the magazine and the chamber.

The PPK was jammed.

The plane was diving again. The lieutenant lost his balance and fell backwards, with George on top of him. The fight in the cockpit was brutal.

George was wrestling with the lieutenant on the floor. The radioman and the engineer were trying to pin down his arms. The engineer was pummeling his head repeatedly with a heavy flare gun. The radioman was kicking him in the kidneys. Blood was running from his head blurring his vision. The fight for Doktor's gun became a life or death fight. Charlie crawled into the cockpit, only to have his leg broken instantly, as the radioman jumped on it. The plane was climbing again, and Charlie, screaming in pain, rolled out of the cockpit, back into the passenger cabin.

George was still in a fight for his life and everyone else. Bolla managed to get into the cockpit. He knocked out the radioman, but the engineer hit him full in the face with the flare gun and Bolla fell backwards, right on top of the still screaming Charlie.

Another nose-dive.

Meanwhile, I was floating with the debris mixed with unconscious passengers, struggling to get to the cockpit. I was crawling over floating obstacles including Charlie's body flat across the doorway, on my way to the cockpit.

George, ignoring the vicious pounding on his head, kept fighting for Doktor's gun with his free hand. He reached it, and wrapped his fingers around the barrel. He was able to get enough leverage to twist it with all his strength. The lieutenant was still holding the butt of the gun with his index finger squeezing the trigger. It was now a matter of wills who would get the gun. George freed his right arm and delivered a powerful blow to Doktors' head, while with his other hand, he kept twisting the barrel. Doktor's body went limp, lost his grip on the gun. George slowly dragged the gun toward his own belly. He felt the locked up position of the top mechanism. He realized that the gun was jammed, and knew exactly what to do.

Still lying on the floor, taking heavy blows to his head, he pushed the button on the side of the handle of the PPK. The magazine dropped halfway down. He reloaded the gun, pushed the magazine back into position, released the top, and heard the clean, clicking sound of the mechanism. Inch by inch, he moved the gun out from underneath his stomach, over to his right side. He rolled over just enough to get the gun in the clear slowly raised the barrel aimed at the engineer's heart, then changed his mind, aimed to the ceiling above the engineer's shoulder, and pulled the trigger.

CHAPTER XVI

The Cockpit of Flight 387 at 200 Feet over Hungary
Friday, July 13, 1956 at 1500 Hour

J UST AS GEORGE PULLED THE TRIGGER, THE PILOTS FLATTENED OUT THE VIOLENT BOUNCING OF THE DC-3 AND HEADED FOR A WHEAT FIELD BEHIND A SMALL FOREST. BANKING TO THE RIGHT AND LEVELING OFF, THE PLANE WAS READY TO CRASH LAND.

"Wheels are up!" yelled the mechanic still in the cockpit.

When George heard the mechanic's yelling, he fired the second shot, straight into the ceiling. This second explosion of the shot in the small cockpit went off with devastating psychological effect. The crew realized that the fight was over.

"Stop shooting! Stop shooting!" yelled Captain Saros.

"We give up! We give up!" yelled the first officer, throwing his hands above his head.

George was standing with one foot on the head of the semiconscious, moaning AVO man. I was already behind him. Smoke was still trailing from the gun's barrel when he shoved it into Captain Saros' ear.

"Pull her up or I'll blow your head off!"

The wheat field was already beneath the plane, it was obvious they were heading for a belly-landing, still about twenty-five miles inside of Hungary.

The barrel was hurting Captain Saros' ear. He knew that the man on the other end of the gun was dead serious. He powered up the engines. The DC-3 was shaking, hesitating with her tilted wingtip; it first leveled off fully, then the nose slowly began to angle upward, and she began to climb. After that, things inside of the aircraft started to calm down, it seemed that the remainder of the flight would be rather uneventful.

The crew, with the exception of the captain, was escorted out of the cockpit at gunpoint. Charlie took the PPK and kept tight aim on them. George took to the controls, occupying the co-pilot's chair. The engines were at full throttle, the plane a couple of hundred feet above the ground. I was standing behind him, wiping the blood still dripping from his head, rolling into his face. George wanted to stay "below the radar" while over Hungary. The Iron Curtain was not in sight yet. The altitude of the flight was so low that George had to tip one wing or another to avoid church steeples, as they seemed to be rushing at the plane. Captain Saros was definitely uncomfortable with George's kamikaze flying. About ten minutes into the revised flight plan, he was the first to see it, then spitting out the words whether with relief that the hugging-the-treetops-flying could come to an end, or maybe with just final resignation:

"There it is!"

And there it was for real: the Iron Curtain. It was coming up fast in the front, slightly to the left of the aircraft. I noticed a cleared up knoll on the Hungarian side of the barbed wire structure with a machinegun tower. A group of soldiers, most likely border AVH, were sitting in a half circle. There could have been a couple dozen of them. In the center, standing, gesticulating with his arms stood an officer, apparently holding a class for the soldiers seated. When the plane came into his sight, the officer was frantically reaching for his sidearm. By the time his hand reached around, I lost his sight. The engines of the DC-3 were roaring, we were leaving him with his side arm, the soldiers, and the land where the sun never seemed to rise, way behind us, forever.

We were over Austria now.

In the early stage of our planning we decided not to land in Austria. For the price of her recently acquired neutrality and freedom from ALL occupational forces, it was hard to guess what concessions the Austrian government would make to the Russians, including a possible arrest and extradition to Hungary. Our destination was West Germany, over two maybe three hundred miles to the west.

George calculated the heading at 285°. Our only navigational aid was a pocket map I had, showing the whole of Europe about the size of a man's palm. There was no communication with any navigational reference source in the air or on the ground.

I walked back to the passenger cabin. Some people were moaning others were silent. I tried to pull the ripped open door as tight as I could. It was impossible to shut it fully: the latching mechanism had been damaged during the violent maneuvering of the plane. I tightened the door handles as much as I could with a belt to keep the door from flopping then began checking the passengers for injuries. As far as I could tell, there were no fatalities or life-threatening injuries. The violent bouncing of the plane caused some of the injuries to passengers already knocked unconscious by us. The uncontrollably sliding heavy cable containing crates have done damage to the interior of the plane as well as to people. (See enclosed photographs) I found an unbroken bottle of apricot brandy in Joe's bag and started pouring it over some open wounds, while freeing people from underneath crates and spilled aluminum cables.

Anais' leg was fractured. She was drifting in and out of consciousness; she must have been in a lot of pain. She opened her eyes, looked up with a smile and asked:

"We made it, sweetheart, didn't we?"

I nodded my head reassuringly.

"Sure we did," I said "Sure we did."

The truth was, I had no idea.

CHAPTER XVII

Soviet airbase Papa, Hungary
Friday, July 13, 1956 at 1500 Hour

A s Captain Bazilevskaya's MIG 17 lifted off the runway, he immediately made a sharp turn, brought his plane into a right bank to check to see if the rest of the wing was with him. When he saw the two other MIG's were airborne, he leveled off at an altitude of three thousand feet. He headed north, and radioed the base for instructions.

"Vulture One to Starbase!"

"Starbase here!" It was Colonel Probishenko himself on the other end, with orders:

"Vulture One, head north. Execute north-south sweeps at three thousand. When you reach the Danube, execute a 180 and head south sixty miles. At the Raba another 180 north."

"Vulture One acknowledged."

In four minutes, the unit reached the Danube. North of the river was Czechoslovakia, no need to look for Flight 387 there, definitely hostile territory if they're trying to escape from behind the Iron Curtain, of which Bazilevskaya was now fully convinced. He made a sharp left, executed a tight 180, and headed south. When he made his second northerly turn, to his left wing he could clearly see the Iron Curtain, less than five miles to the west. It was a clear day, though farther to the west above the Alps thunderheads were gathering. Two minutes into the northerly sweep, he spotted the DC-3. She was approximately forty miles to the west, at least twenty-five miles into Austria, flying lower than a thousand feet, heading for the Alps.

"The son of a bitch," he swore and contacted the base.

"Vulture One to Starbase. The goony bird is thirty miles into Austrian airspace, heading at 285. Requesting permission to pursue."

First, he thought that Starbase did not hear him, because it was such a long pause.

But then came the voice of the Colonel, slow, subdued:

"Starbase to Vulture One: negative."

After another short pause,

"Negative. Return to Starbase."

Captain Bazilevskaya shook his head then banked sharply to the right.

Fifteen minutes later the wheels of his MIG-17 hit the tarmac at the air base. Two minutes later all three MIG's were on the ground.

OVER THE ALPS

CHAPTER XVIII

Over the Austrian Alps

OR ABOUT FIFTEEN MINUTES WE WERE FLYING ACCORDING TO OUR PLANS, 285° WEST. Below, a large river to the right, it had to be the Danube, we thought. The plan was to follow the river to Regensburg, then turn south and land in Munich or anywhere as long as it's an airport in West Germany. We passed by the south side of a huge city, which must have been Vienna, flying at a relatively safe altitude, with an aircraft having a door to the outside that could not be closed.

While the ceiling for the DC-3 was officially quoted as 26,000 feet, we climbed only to half of that: 13,000 feet.

Captain Saros, resigned to the fact that the plane was in our control, with George calling the shots, became cooperative, almost jovial. He said if they flew much higher there could be problems with the aircraft's structural stability, not to mention the need for pressurization for the passengers, especially considering what they just went through. He and

George agreed to maintain 13,000 feet altitude, and for a short while peace settled in the aircraft. Then things began to change, this time on the outside. From the southwest, heavy cumuli-nimbus clouds were rolling in, bringing towering thunderheads moving north. The river that was supposed to be our major landmark and navigational aid had disappeared beneath the clouds. Both pilots now shared a common interest: avoid crashing into the mountains. They began dodging the darkening clouds, looking for holes of visibility. Then the thunderheads melted into one solid grayish soup, obscuring everything beyond the wing tips.

"What do you know about the Alps?" Saros asked George, trying to maintain a calm voice with little success.

George was still George:

"Me? Everything. I fly over here almost every day, didn't you know?" he answered sarcastically.

"Should we change course a bit north, say to 330°?" asked Saros.

Of course George knew better. Any change to the north/northwest direction would surely land us in Czechoslovakia. Hardly a choice. A Communist controlled country under the yoke of the Soviets. As far as we were concerned it was as bad, if not worse, than a crash landing in Hungary.

"Still looking for your comrades on the ground?" George asked.

"Just trying to stay alive but the odds look worse by the minute," said Saros.

George had no answer. It was obvious that only God had one, but unfortunately with Him there was no communication at the present. I was standing next to George, occasionally wiping the slowly trickling blood out of his eyes. Flying blind because of the clouds was bad enough; having blurred vision due to dripping blood did not make it any better.

"Can you see?" I asked him.

"What is there to see?" his response was more of a frustrated question than an answer.

That was true, there was nothing to see, and George's answer brought more fear into my heart. I loved geography while in school. My teacher used to tell the class, "If you can't find a place on the map ask Zak. If he doesn't know where it is, it may not even exist, let alone be on the map." In those days, a decade back, it sounded funny. Now it was anything but funny. I knew enough about the Alps, including the Austrian Alps. They did not have the highest elevation of the Alp, that was Mount Blanc in Switzerland. But there were plenty of peaks in the Austrian Alps towering around 10,000 feet or above. The white grayish soup and those mean looking rolling pillows, passing by as clouds, made the sky look as if it was sick, ready to throw up. I could see the props cutting the clouds into messy slices, only to be reassembled instantaneously. I could see the wing tips only sporadically.

The fear in the cockpit was heavy. I reached over my heart trying to monitor my heartbeat, but to no avail. I counted the beats up to twenty, maybe thirty, then realized I had no watch to measure the beats against the time.

"What's the use anyway?!"

The clouds got heavier and darker as time went by.

I tried to imagine the impact. What I would feel if the plane crashed head on into the mountain or what if we just hit one huge rock with one of the wings? I wished that we would hit head-on, with no time to think, and no pain; we would just be gone.

"George, can't we go higher?" I pleaded.

It seemed to be an eternity before George answered:

"Settle down, do your praying!"

More than an hour later, still flying in the soup, Saros turned to George,

"Can we bring in the engineer?"

George did not respond. Saros added what I was afraid to hear.

"I think we need to start landing; we're running out of fuel."

George still had not said a word. Instead, he slowly began to execute landing procedures. The nose of the DC-3 tilted down sharply. The plane was descending at a rapid rate. I had that sickening feeling again, my stomach rising into my throat.

"It's going to happen now," I thought, forcing my eyelids shut, and started to play my "death game." It went like this: if we don't crash by the time I count to a hundred, we're safe."

Yeah, dream on… I started counting again. Once I passed fifty, I accelerated the count, as if I could get to one hundred faster, the critical number of safety in my game. I counted to one hundred five times before we broke out of the cloud-cover.

The rolling soup of death was now above us. As I looked through the left side of the cockpit window a forest came into view below the plane.

And there was, oh God—there was sunshine!

Just as in a dream, to the right, below us, was a runway. A real runway, maybe four kilometers long. The concrete of the runway looked as if it had been recently poured, but there was nothing else, just a runway. No hangars, no planes, no control tower, not even a windsock. We were already passing over the runway.

"Nothing more useless than a runway behind you when you need to land," said George calmly.

The engineer was in the cockpit. The pilots pulled up the plane, headed straight out about six miles, then banking hard to the left, re-approached the runway from the opposite end. They were guessing the prevailing wind and its speed, they guessed right; we were landing into some light wind. The engineer cranked the wheels down. The sun peeked out behind scattered clouds witnessing a historic event.

When the wheels of HA- LIG Flight 387 touched the concrete of the runway, we still had no idea in which country we had landed.

CHAPTER XIX

THE RUNWAY WAS COMPLETELY DESERTED, NOT A SOUL IN SIGHT. I TOOK THE PPK FROM CHARLIE AND CHECKED IT. THERE WERE FOUR BULLETS LEFT IN THE MAGAZINE AND ONE IN THE CHAMBER.

UNSCHEDULED LANDING

CHAPTER XX

An unknown runway in an unknown country
Friday, July 13, 1956 at 1855 Hour

KARL MEYER WAS 55 YEARS OLD AND LIVED IN MANCHING, A SMALL CITY NEAR INGOLSTADT, LOCATED IN THE FEDERAL REPUBLIC OF GERMANY, AKA WEST GERMANY. Karl and his wife usually spent their Friday afternoons walking in the forest near the city. During summer, when mushrooms or berries were in season, they spent hours in the forest before going home around sunset. Karl sometimes came later in the day because he had to make deliveries. Driving his bicycle, he would then try to catch up with his wife who started out earlier in the day. By mid-afternoon, they usually were together having a late lunch, with Karl enjoying a beer or two afterwards.

A year or so ago, the American occupational forces based in Ingolstadt were out in Manching, near the big forest, with bulldozers and all kinds of construction equipment. The word was that this would someday be a NATO airbase. As far as Karl was concerned, NATO was just another name for the Americans. Not that he had anything against them, on the contrary. The construction stayed away from the trees, which he appreciated. The tarmac laid down a few months ago was about three hundred feet from the edge of the forest.

It was July 13, 1956 and Karl and his wife were spending their Friday as usual. They finished their lunch and went on picking berries. This time it was raspberry season and there were plenty. The wife filled up her basket way before sunset. Karl was leisurely pushing his bicycle. There was no hurry to get home; dinner would not be until after eight. It was about half past six, the sun still high on the horizon. It looked like just another peaceful Friday. Karl and his wife rested at the edge of the forest with the vacant airstrip in front of them.

Then things changed…

As far as Karl knew, no plane had ever landed on this long runway, not yet. According to his understanding, the base was planning to open it the next year with a ceremony of some sort. That no longer seemed to be the case. Out of the eastern end of the runway, a two-engine plane roared into view flying a few hundred feet above the trees. At first glance, Karl thought it was a private plane. What else could it be? But then he realized that it was far too big for a private plane. Instead of landing, it seemed to hesitate, lumbering, perhaps even thinking, *"Should I or should I not land here."* The sound of the props roared into a higher pitch, the plane started into a slow climb, flying over the western end of the runway higher than it came in.

The plane, instead of disappearing, did a one-eighty about six kilometers out, then headed back again toward the runway. This time the plane landed. Karl and his wife stood staring at the plane, which was rolling, then slowing down a few hundred feet from where they were standing. The plane was still moving slowly in a halfway circle facing the western end of the runway turning toward Ingolstadt. Finally it came to a full stop. Then it just sat there, nothing was happening. The props were still twirling at a high rate of speed.

The door of the plane apparently was on the right side of the fuselage the opposite side of where Karl stood, out of his view. Then he saw a pair of legs in long, black pants dangling from the plane. Apparently, someone was climbing down. Then the legs gave way to hips and torso; he could see almost the whole person hanging from the plane. Finally he jumped, landed on the ground and rolled sideways then got up, shook himself, and started to walk around toward the back of the plane. He came around the tail from the other side, and while looking around, spotted the couple. The stranger stopped in his tracks, seemed to hesitate, then began to walk toward Karl and his wife.

The man seemed to be relatively young with a nice clean face. He was wearing a black pair of pants, and some shoes that looked like tennis shoes. A short-sleeved shirt that once upon a time must have been white was now covered in huge patches of red blood smeared all over. The man from the plane was only about twenty feet away, when Karl's wife panicked and started to run away. In the hurry she dropped the basket, full of raspberries.

Karl Meyer decided to stand his ground.

He placed the bicycle sideways in front of him like a shield, just in case.

***

When the plane finally came to a stop, I was the only one on the team with no broken bones, could walk still and spoke reasonable German. Charlie spoke fluent German but he had a broken leg. I had to find the answer to the still life or death question: what country are we in?

There were a number of possibilities as to where we could have landed, not all of them pleasant: East Germany, although it was too far to the north, then the real possibilities were Czechoslovakia, Austria, or our hope—West Germany. A neutral Austria was a huge question, whether they would return everybody to the Hungarian "authorities" in order to keep their "neutrality" intact in the eyes of the Kremlin. These were hard choices, but I had to face them. If Czechoslovakia, I'll shoot Anais and then myself.

But will I have the strength?

If it's Austria, I'll take my chances.

But again, it may be the dream of freedom: West Germany, with the Americans.

I was going through this in my mind as I was untying the loose door of the DC-3 and began climbing down from the plane. The stairs built into the door were nonfunctional. My feet were dangling from the plane as I was slowly sliding down. At the end, I was holding on to the frame of the fuselage right where the bottom of the door should have been. I let go of the edge of the doorframe, and a second later landed softly on the tarmac. My knees buckled upon impact, I ended up on my left side. I rose, shook my shoulders, my legs. They were all OK.

The runway was deserted. Only the deep black color of the tarmac indicated that it was brand new, unused or not-yet-used, rather than old and abandoned.

I walked around the back of the aircraft, came out on the opposite side, and looked toward the forest a couple of hundred feet away. Then I spotted two people, a man and a woman at the edge of the forest.

They were standing still, facing the plane. I hesitated for a moment before I started walking toward them. They were still motionless. I raised my right arm in a greeting motion, trying to make it a friendly one. The pistol was in my pants pocket however I had no intention of using it. As I got about half way, I launched into a slow run toward them. They were standing still but just for a few more seconds. When I got closer maybe 20-30 feet, the woman turned around and ran into the forest. The man placed his bike into a defensive position in front of him. While his whole stance looked very solid, his face reflected horror.

Why is he looking at my chest? Then I looked down at my front.

Oh Lord! All that blood from George's head wounds—I came to realize as I slowed my steps, almost tiptoeing toward the man not to scare him. I was racking my brain for a question that wouldn't give me away, but would tell me what I needed to know.

"Adenauer?" (Referring to the Chancellor of West Germany at the time) I asked.

"Nein, Ich bin kein Adenauer" (No, I am not Adenauer)

Ask a stupid question, you'll get a stupid answer—I thought, *let's try again!*

"Bonn?" I asked now referring to the capital of West Germany.

"Nein," said the man again somewhat irritated. Frozen by fear of getting an answer I'd rather not hear, I was running out of patience with all this beating around the bush asking the big one that I foolishly thought to be the all-deciding one.

"Communist?"

The man looked at me then waved his arm, lifted his bike, turned around, and started to walk away. I never felt so stupid in my life. Hopelessly frustrated with my own inability to establish the truth I was afraid of. Also feeling foolish embarrassed.

Why couldn't I just ask a straight question? I thought to myself, like: *'Hello brother is this West Germany or what?'*

It was too late; the man was gone.

About a hundred feet away he stopped, looked back then continued into the forest. Probably to find the woman who ran away.

I headed back to the plane.

Members of our team who were still able to walk, Joe, George, Gabor, and I, put together makeshift slides using floorboards, and began to ease the remaining passengers off the plane. In about ten minutes everyone, except the crew, was unloaded, laying or sitting around on the grass near the runway.

HOME, SWEET HOME

Chapter XXI

T HAT'S WHEN IT ALL BEGAN TO HAPPEN. At the end of the runway a car appeared. The murmur of the passengers on the grassy knoll faded into heavy silence. Some members of our team slowly began to rise. I glanced over to Anais, just a couple of feet away from me slid my hand into my pocket, holding on to the PPK.

The car seemed to be moving in super slow motion.

Suddenly it was there.

My feet trembled. My body was shaking like a fallen leaf in the autumn wind. Tears filled my eyes and streamed down my face. Through those tear-filled eyes, through my blurred vision, the sight was unmistakably clear. Blown by the gentle afternoon breeze coming from the west, on the antenna of the car, there it was;

THE STARS AND STRIPES.

***

Jimmy B., originally from Alabama, a corporal with the US Army providing security for the Manching NATO airbase near Ingolstadt in West Germany, was on a routine inspection drive of the airport which was under construction about eighty miles from of the Czechoslovakian border. As he drove up the road parallel with the runway, he confronted the most unexpected scene: a DC-3 parked on the tarmac. First he stopped his Jeep then drove up onto the runway approaching the plane. About a hundred feet from the plane he stopped again, rose from the driver's seat and stepped halfway on the running board of his vehicle.

He heard the sound of a siren, actually more than one—from the western end of the runway: ambulances, he thought and as he turned halfway, he could see the flashing red lights on at least two of them, racing toward the DC3 .

But the scene - a rather stunning one—was played out right in front of his Jeep. On the grass, next to the runway's tarmac, sat a group of people, mostly men. As they spotted the Jeep, three or four of them— they seemed to be rather young and, to his relief, not at all hostile— staggered to their feet and begun to approach his vehicle.

A strange group it was.

Some were dragging their feet, another's arm was hanging limp by his side. One of them, in a bloodied shirt, kept looking at the antenna of the Jeep, and as he got next to the car, fell on his knees, and put his arms around the wheel.

It was surreal, almost ritualistic. In the meantime one of the ambulances arrived, and they started to examine people, while the other was maneuvering around the DC3 to another group. The people in front of the Jeep were not moving.

"Who are you people?" asked the corporal.

The one, in the bloodied shirt straightened up, pointed toward the DC3 when he said:

"Hungarian, freedom!" and he collapsed back on the Jeep's fender.

"Holy shit" said the corporal as he reached for his shortwave radio.

It was 18:55PM by Greenwich Mean Time on July 13, 1956, Friday.

***

Being July, the sun was still high in the sky, far from setting on the western horizon. I looked up to the sun, squinting. I could swear that the sun was visibly rising.

Anais looked up to me and in her whispering voice, as if reading my mind, she asked: "Is that the sun rising?"

"Yes honey, it is," I was not lying. For seven just-liberated slaves, the sun had risen for the second time that day. This time in the West.

She closed her eyes, probably to subdue the pain and whispered.

"Where are we?"

I looked at the flag gently waiving from the antenna of the Jeep and the answer came from the depth of my heart, from a depth I did not know existed.

"Sweetheart, we are home!"

Then I kissed her gently.

EPILOGUE

Freedom Flight, the escape of Flight 387 from Communist controlled Hungary is a true story, narrated with as much accuracy as one could recall from the distance of more than a half century.

The story attempts to present a historical account of a series of dramatic events, all of which in fact took place. The escape is documented by media accounts with selected copies enclosed. Events that took place in my absence—the activities on the Russian airbase at Papa, the coincidental timing for the removal of Rakosi on the same day—all have been reconstructed from historical archives or testimonies of reliable witnesses.

***

The events at the Soviet airbase at Papa, the dispatch of the MIG 17s.

Four months after my escape, the Hungarian Revolution rocked the "Soviet Empire". While the Soviets and their Hungarian slave masters eventually returned to power, several thousands, estimated to be a quarter of a million, escaped, while the Iron Curtain was unattended for about three weeks. I lived in the free section of Germany (West Germany at the time) and worked for a western intelligence agency. I had the opportunity to meet a wide variety of refugees escaping Hungary before the Iron Curtain rang down again. They were transitioning through Germany to whatever their final destination was. My good fortune was meeting Laszlo. Before escaping, Laszlo worked as a maintenance engineer at the Russian air force base at Papa and was delighted to give me finite details of virtually every minute that occurred after the base was alerted to the "disappearance" of HA-LIG, Flight 387. He told me that a "MAYDAY" call, followed by "we are attempting an emergency landing" from the flight's cockpit, led to the order of the MIG 17s to pursue. He also knew that the jets came back from a failed mission less than thirty minutes later. Although details of the failed mission were supposed to be kept secret, the base was buzzing with the details of the pursuit and the eventual abortion of the mission. He said he knew the lead pilot personally. The fact that he (Laszlo) spoke fluent Russian attributed to the credibility of his story.

***

Reconstructed from the archives of historical documents

The coincidental, behind the scenes, meeting for the final removal of Matyas Rakosi, Stalin's Hungarian surrogate at the time, is duly recorded in the archives of that era and presented in this book only as a background reference.

The imposing building of the Soviet embassy on Bajza Street in Budapest was the headquarters for Yuri Andropov, the Soviet Ambassador to Hungary, a high level KGB man. After Stalin's death, his ruthless henchman, Lavrentij Pavlovic Berija became the Secretary of the Politburo, the ultimate authority of the Soviet Union. Andropov had his reservations about Berija's elevation. Sure enough, in a rather short time Berija fell out of favor. He was actually killed by his faithful comrades at a Politburo session. Just a few years later, Andropov's star began to rise, he was convinced that one day he would sit at the chairman's seat in the Politburo.

He also knew that the road to that coveted chair was long, with no room for mistakes. Not even a slight one. Challenges were plenty. The ambassadorship to Hungary was one of those challenging stopovers. The bulk of the Hungarian intelligentsia had escaped as the Soviet steamroller headed west a decade earlier. Most of them ended up in parts of Europe under American occupation, some eventually moved to America. Others escaped when they saw Communism coming. They evaporated before the Iron Curtain was built. As mentioned earlier, Tolbuchin rounded up a hundred thousand or so Hungarians, and had them shipped to the Gulags, to save himself from Stalin's wrath for the stall at Budapest during World War II. All that was left, as far as Andropov was concerned, were gypsies.

Now it was 1956 and the natives were restless in Hungary. Students at universities were forming "activity clubs" with the ostensible purpose of social advancement and searching for "their roots." Three years earlier the Kremlin ordered the sectional privatization of the farmlands in Hungary, which reverted about ten percent of the state-owned, collective farm system into private ownership. The move worked, at least on the surface. Then a fatal mistake was made by Matyas Rakosi, the Hungarian replica of Stalin, relentlessly trying to equal the brutality of his master. By 1955 he convinced enough members of the Politburo in Moscow to pull the plug on the Hungarian privatization program of the farm system after two short years.

As it turned out, it was too early.

Andropov knew it but his pleading with the Kremlin went unheeded. In early 1955, the Central Committee of the Hungarian Communist Party put an end to the privatization scheme, thus plunging the short-lived hopes and dreams of millions of Hungarians back into darkness. The privatization was declared an imperialist conspiracy by revisionist members of the Party. Imre Nagy was removed from his position, and the gulags that in previous years were on the decline were reinstituted again.

Matyas Rakosi was restored to full power as the Secretary of the Hungarian Communist Party's Central Committee with power over life and death. Andropov knew that Rakosi's number would be up inevitably, just a matter of time. Hungary began to show the unmistakable signs of the restlessness of slaves occupying a totally mismanaged country. Andropov began to communicate the danger signals to Moscow; the same members of the Politburo, who supported Rakosi a year before, were ready to change their minds.

It was just a matter of time.

Rakosi had no inkling as to what was going on in the Kremlin, and while in early 1956 the decision was already made about his removal, not a single member of the Politburo "spilled the beans". His calls and reports were responded to by the Kremlin just as before, so as not to alert him unduly. While he was confident of his security at Moscow, however mistakenly, things were not going too well at home. Industrial production dropped dangerously low, quotas were not met for the delivery of railroad engines, busses, agricultural machinery, bauxite (the raw material for aluminum, one of the few real natural resource of Hungary). All of this production was retribution for Hungary's role against the Soviets in World War II and it was in serious disarray.

Rakosi instituted the usual tactics of remedy, ratcheting up what he knew best, terror. Factory managers were arrested and workers were forced to work overtime for some meaningless medals, instead of real pay. Production quotas were raised, and by early 1956 the technique seemed to work except in two distinct areas, both of which were heavy industrial venues. There were even rumblings about striking, the word considered a capital sin in the Communist economic system.

On July 13, 1956, Anastas Mikoyan, member of the Politburo of the Soviet Union, arrived in Budapest. The purpose of the trip was to remove Matyas Rakosi and transport him to an asylum in Moscow.

Incurable illness, like in the case of many of his Communist predecessors, was to be diagnosed. Consequently it was to be declared that no local medical institution had either the technology, or could be trusted with the life and health of such an important person as Rakosi. The designated place was a sanatorium in Moscow specifically designed for the treatment of deposed party functionaries.

The removal needed to be handled with kid gloves: Mikoyan was the right person to do it. The steps were routine: Rakosi was to announce the discovery of a terminal illness. Mikoyan was there to offer the advanced medical assistance of the Soviet Union. Rakosi was to resign from the Central Committee and with assistance from Hungary's great friend, Moscow, to find his (forever) resting place in the Soviet Union.

What did all these facts have to do with our escape?

The word on Rakosi's removal was rumored already in early July. The arrival of Mikoyan on July 13, 1956, Friday had thrown the entire Hungarian security system—Rakosi's very own elite political terror force, the AVO—into frenzy days before. The system that ensured that nobody could feel safe, not even in the highest levels of the hierarchy, including its own, now had its chickens coming home to roost. They all were running to save their own hides. Absolutely no attention was paid by anyone at the AVO as to what was going on locally, security-wise. Had there been any attentiveness, it should have been screamingly obvious to the security forces that something was very odd: seven Hungarian "students" bought airline tickets to a Hungarian border city.

Airline tickets? In 1956, in Hungary?

What's wrong with traveling on a train? Where did they get the money? Why was a woman, 20 years old, flying? Airlines were reserved for party functionaries and important company executives. Tickets were supposed to be purchased through state security approved agencies!

What was going on?

An unforgivable, unexplainable mistake by one of the world's most effectively operated secret police with no other excuse than the diverted attention: the fear created by the visit of Mikoyan. The question preempted any security consideration: whose heads will roll when the inevitable fall of Rakosi finally happens?

The Almighty State had fallen on its own sword and was invincible no longer.

SERENDIPITY

The day the stars lined up...

REVIEWING THE EVENTS OF THE ESCAPE FROM THE DISTANCE OF OVER A HALF CENTURY, IT'S BEYOND A SHADOW OF A DOUBT THAT CHANCES FOR ITS SUCCESS WERE ASTRONOMICALLY SMALL. Certain, totally unorthodox, events needed to happen in a precise sequence at an exact time in order to synergistically improve the chances of the escape, and even then, the chances for success remained miniscule.

Let's look at some of these "stars":

George, the team leader

In my opinion, no other person amongst the thousands of acquaintances I have met throughout my life would ever be able to conduct such a superhuman fight against five crewmembers, (one of them armed) as did George in the cockpit of the DC-3.

The cockpit door

The aircraft of Flight 387 that day was the only one of six aircrafts owned by MALEV (Hungarian Air Transport Co.) that had a plywood cockpit door. All others had doors made of aluminum making the prying open of the door impossible (see enclosed photograph).

The malfunctioning firearm

Misfiring of a handgun, as it happened in the hand of the AVO agent, is a rare event. The AVO security man assigned to the flight for the purpose of preventing a take-over of control related his story later, during interrogation by his superiors in Budapest. (Translated copy of the AVO agent, D.E.'s testimony enclosed).

The critical thirty seconds

The missing thirty seconds the pilots needed to belly -land the aircraft on a wheat field inside Hungary. The aircraft was less than 500 feet from crash-landing when George got possession of the AVO agent's gun and the control of the aircraft. Had either of the pilots decided to belly-land the plane anyway, they could have been successful, in which case the plane would never take off again. (Testimony of GJ chief pilot).

No death or serious (permanent) injuries

Most of the injuries, including those suffered by the "team" resulted from the violent bouncing of the aircraft. In addition, in a typically uncaring fashion, large wooden crates—three or four of them—containing heavy aluminum cables, were stored on the aisle of the plane unsecured. As the aircraft started its dives and sharp climbs, these crates became airborne missiles knocking everything in their path. Miraculously the injuries caused by these flying heavy objects were relatively light.

The missed move by the AVO agent

One of several critically missed moves was the AVO agent's refusal to fire into the cockpit door while George was prying it open from the other side; in spite of being asked to fire by another crew member. He (the AVO agent) claimed during interrogation that he had only one magazine of bullets and he wanted to save them for the anticipated gun battle (DE testimony, enclosed).

The fatally wrong decision by the AVO agent

The decision by the AVO agent to station himself in the cockpit rather than in the passenger cabin, as protocol requested, was a bad move. Had he been in the passenger section of the aircraft, his chances of using his firearm would have been infinitely better, possibly killing George before he could break into the cockpit.

The removal of the Hungarian despot, Matyas Rakosi, on the same day

After ten years in power, the Kremlin decided to dump their Hungarian surrogate, Rakosi. The date of doing so was decided to be July 13, 1956. The hierarchy of the Communist power structure, both Hungarian and Soviet in Budapest at that date, was preoccupied with the handling of the "Rakosi Issue". This "preoccupation" included Yuri Andropov, Soviet Ambassador to Hungary and Anastas Mikoyan, member of the Politburo who was assigned to handle the issue, visiting Budapest the same day.

AVO is the acronym for the Allamvedelmi Osztaly (Authority for the Protection of the State), the Hungarian version of the KGB or the Stasi and equally brutal to their Soviet or East German counterparts. In fact, it was the AVO that exercised uncontrolled, unlimited power over life and death in Hungary. Their excesses in brutality were simply beyond description.

EVENTS IN HUNGARY DURING
AND FOLLOWING THE ESCAPE

July 13, 1956, Friday, Budapest, Ferihegy airport at 1418 Hour a domestic MALEV flight: HA-LIG Flight 387 takes off for Szombathely and on to Zalaegerszeg ten minutes late.

July 13, 1956, Friday, in the airspace of Szil (Hungary) at 1453 Hour Flight 387 sends a MAYDAY signal: "We are preparing to execute an emergency landing."

July 13, 1956, Friday, Manching, Federal Republic of Germany (West-Germany) at 1849 Hour Flight 387 lands at a NATO airbase still under construction.

July 14, 1956, Saturday, Budapest, Hungary. Total confusion and chaos at the AVO reigned. The Interior Affairs Ministry, the arm of the government responsible for the activities of the AVO, tortures, executions, trials, etc., resorted to monitoring western radio broadcasts to learn what happened to Flight 387. They learned from the front-page story of the New York Times, published on July 14, 1956, that Flight 387 was diverted and landed in Manching West Germany. An "Operative Plan" was constructed immediately and investigations began.

July 14, 1956 through July 21, Hungary. The AVO conducts an intensive background search of the relatives, friends and acquaintances of the seven members of the "team" referring to them throughout as "air gangsters".

July 21, 1956, Hegyeshalom, a border-crossing town between Austria and Hungary.

The return of five passengers and the crew of five. An elaborate reception was held by state authorities followed by "de-briefing" of all passengers and the crew. A West German reporter was traveling with the convoy with the intention of interviewing the relatives of the escapees. The AVO continued to divert his attempts until he finally gave up and returned to Germany without accomplishing his assignment.

July 21 through Aug 16, 1956

Interrogation of passengers and crew.

Elaborate records of the interrogations were produced, illustrating the incredibly complex and invasive structure of the police state. All crewmembers turned out to be either built in informers, or close relatives in high positions of the oppressive power structure. The brother of the chief pilot was a major in the AVO. Not only was the crew of the flight organized into the system of reporting of any suspicious activities, three of the five returning passengers also turned out to be "AVO operatives" even though they had regular jobs.

July 23, 1956. An international warrant was issued for the arrest of all the escapees, whose whereabouts were identified as Ingolstadt, West Germany. The authority to prosecute the case was transferred to the Hungarian Department of Justice, ostensibly having broader jurisdictional authority, including requesting extradition of the "criminals" under international law.

July 25, 1956. The Supreme Military Command of Budapest established three different crimes according to the Hungarian Criminal Codes, two of which, damaging of state property and treason, were punishable by death. All the escapees were subject to the death penalty upon arrest and/or capture (report enclosed).

October 13, 1956. A similar escape attempt was made on the same regularly scheduled flight between Budapest, Szombathely, and Zalaegerszeg on Oct 13, 1956. According to reports, five Hungarian youths developed an escape plan fashioned after the July 13, 1956 successful escape. Preparations for the escape were discovered by the AVO in advance. The group boarded the aircraft in Szombathely for the short flight to Zalaegerszeg. Unbeknownst to the group, the leader was arrested before he could board the plane. Eight minutes into the flight the remaining four members made their move. The AVO agents were prepared, posing as passengers.

The escapees pulled their weapons, including a submachine gun they were successful in smuggling on-board, however the AVO agents were faster and gunned down two of the escapees. One escapee died on board, another was fatally injured; the remaining two were arrested, and their fate is unknown to the author.

October 23, 1956. The Hungarian Revolution erupted against the Communist regime.

The increasing oppression of human rights, along with the naked terror by the AVO resulted in a full-scale uprising known as the Hungarian Revolution of 1956. Thousands, many of them teenagers, died while battling superior Soviet forces in Budapest. Finally, in early November 1956, the Soviets moved in with full force and brought the fight of freedom that lasted for 19 days to a tragic end: extending the Soviet oppression for 33 additional years.

Throughout the three weeks while the country was out of Soviet control, several hundred thousand Hungarians escaped to the West, taking advantage of the opened borders. By mid-November 1956, the Iron Curtain was firmly re-established, allowing for no more escapes.

DOCUMENTS OF AN
IMPOSSIBLE DREAM

DOCUMENTS

(Translated from Hungarian)
The Supreme Prosecutor's Office
Extremely Secret For Special Cases
Subject: P. George and accompanying criminals' act
Case # 1956 BUL 002692
To the President of the Military Tribunal
Budapest Division, Budapest

THE HUNGARIAN COMMERCIAL AIR CO.'S FLIGHT, IDENTIFIED AS HA-LIG, COMMUTING BETWEEN BUDAPEST SZOMBATHELY AND ZALAEGERSZEG ON ITS REGULARLY SCHEDULED FLIGHT ON JULY 13, 1956, WAS ATTACKED BY AN ORGANIZED AND ARMED GROUP FORCING THE AIRCRAFT TO LAND ON THE TERRITORY OF THE FEDERAL REPUBLIC OF GERMANY.

The consequent investigation determined that members of said group had been preparing for the execution of the above-cited event arming themselves with firearms as well as with other objects. They provoked a fight aboard and eventually overcame the crew of the aircraft, forcing it into the airspace of the Federal Republic of Germany, and were landing in Manching on a US Military airport. Throughout the fight, on board were several—so far unidentified—individuals, who received serious injuries and it caused major damage to the aircraft itself.

(The rest of the document is the enumeration of the crew and passengers of the flight, not directly pertinent to the actual event. The date of the document is July 21, 1956)

HISTORICAL (ARCHIVE) RECORDS OF THE INTERROGATION OF D.E.

TOPIC:

Diversion of MALEV flight identified as HA-LIG Budapest-Szombathely-Zalaegerszeg

Date of Flight: July 13, 1956

Interrogator: C.J. AVO Lieutenant

Subject of interrogation: D.E. Police Lieutenant in service of the AVH transportation security

Date of Report: Aug 16, 1956, Budapest, Hungary

Preamble by the author:

The five returning passengers and the five crew members were "debriefed" by the AVO during the weeks following their return. The testimonies of the subjects of the debriefing were heavily tainted and reflected their fear of being accused, whether proven or not, of complicity with the diversion of

the flight. While all those testimonies are now part of the Archives of the State Security Services, (Állambiztonsági Szolgálatok Történeti Levéltára) the author has elected to use only the testimony of D.E., the AVO agent on the plane, since his description, even though slanted to defend his action or the lack thereof, reflects the closest available narrative of what really went on during the fight, referred to by the media as the "bloody struggle for the control of the aircraft".

NOTE: *The Interrogator shall be identified as C.J.*

C.J. Please tell me how the events of the gangster attack (sic) went down on July 13 aboard the flight identified as HA-LIG.

D.E. I was assigned to provide security on that passenger plane which took off 15 minutes late on its schedule from Budapest to Szombathely. As the aircraft took off, I occupied a seat in the cockpit. As we passed Gyor and approached the airspace over Szil, we heard a suspicious sound, as if someone kicked the cockpit door. T.S., the flight mechanic, and I jumped up immediately and I loaded my pistol, sliding one bullet into the chamber to make it ready to fire. T.S. advised me to stay behind and cover him while he went to investigate the source of the strange sound. He opened the door slightly and yanked it back immediately and yelled at the chief pilot (G.J.) to "Dive hard!" because we were being attacked by people equipped with gun(s). As a result of this warning the chief pilot began to bounce the aircraft very hard, bringing it into deep dives and sharp vertical climbs about three or four times. I kept shifting between being glued to the ceiling and being slammed to the floor by the bouncing. As the aircraft was tossed up and down the door suddenly swung open and a person jumped into the cockpit with a large gun in hand and hit me on the head causing me to fall backwards onto the floor.

C.J. In exactly what position were you when the person jumped in and where was your gun?

D.E. The aircraft was diving when the person jumped in. At this time I was hanging on to some equipment protruding from the ceiling with my left hand while holding the gun in my right hand. As I recall, I pointed the gun at the person, pulled the trigger, but the gun failed to fire. After being hit, I fell backwards and George P. immediately jumped on me and immobilized the wrist of my right hand where I was holding the gun. With my free left hand I grabbed his throat and began to choke him. In the meantime, I was yelling to T.S. to knock him out. He (T.S.) was pounding George P. on the head. In the meantime some other bandit forced his way into the cockpit and I got hit again with a stick. I was dazed for a time and they grabbed my gun out of my hand.

C.J. *When your gun was fired in what position were you?*

D.E. I could not hear the firing of the gun due to the repeated hits on my head. I lost consciousness and when I came to I was lying on the floor and observed that the mechanic T.S., the navigator B.K., and the co-pilot F.J., were no longer in the cockpit. The chief pilot G.J. was sitting in his chair but George P. was already in the seat of the co-pilot. One of the gangsters was holding my own gun to my head.

C.J. *When did you hear that George P. was yelling, "Give up the plane?"*

D.E. I did not hear that.

C.J. *Please continue your testimony*

D.E. When I came to, I had no idea where we were because they did not let me up and I was impaired by the beating I took and the pain I experienced.

C.J. *Who offered you alcohol on the plane?*

D.E. As far as I can remember, one of the gangsters, J.B. offered, but I did not accept. So he, J.B. poured the alcohol on my head with the intent of stopping my bleeding.

C.J. *T.S. told you to shoot through the cockpit door when he realized that you were being attacked, did he not?*

D.E. I heard that someone from the crew was yelling to me to shoot into the door but I did not. T.S. told me they had guns and since I had only one magazine of bullets, I decided to save the bullets for the real gun battle I expected. Later on the passengers commented that someone by the name of T.P. was standing in front of the door and a shot would have hit him had I fired…

C.J. *Continue…*

The rest of D.E.'s testimony deals with the stay in the Ingolstadt hospital and is not relevant as to what happened in the airplane during the takeover of control

EXHIBITS

The New York Times

July 14, 1956: Page 1

7 Seize Hungarian Airliner In Midair Fight, Fly to West

All 19 Aboard Injured as Battle Between Fleeing Students and Reds Breaks Out Again After Plane Lands in Germany

By ARTHUR J. OLSEN

Special to The New York Times.

BONN, Germany, July 13— Seven Hungarian students overpowered the crew of a Hungarian commercial airliner tonight and forced their way at pistol point to freedom in West Germany.

As the plane landed at a half-completed military field at Ingolstadt, Bavaria, a bloody battle between loyalist and defecting Hungarians erupted again.

By the time German policemen broke up the fight, all nineteen occupants of the plane were injured. Twelve were taken to a hospital for treatment.

The seven students, described as between the ages of 19 and 25, were not sure they had made good their bid for freedom until the plane had rolled to a stop on the airstrip outside the Bavarian city. A man with blood streaming down his face threw open the cabin door and shouted to a German workman, "Where are we?"

The workman, Karl Meyer, said the fight was still on in the cabin as he reached the plane.

One of the defectors later gave this account of the successful getaway:

The twin-engine Malev airliner left Budapest in late afternoon with fifteen passengers and four crew members aboard. After a stop at Gyor, it took off for Szombathely, a Hungarian city near the Austrian border.

"About ten minutes after we left Gyor, the leader of our group, a former Hungarian commercial pilot, pulled out an old pistol and hit the man next to him on the head," the university student said.

"This was the signal for the rest of us to pull out iron bars we had concealed in our clothing to try to overpower the other passengers.

"We had a terrific fight. We

Continued on Page 3, Column 7

282

7 STUDENTS SEIZE HUNGARIAN PLANE

Continued From Page 1

knew there was a secret policeman on the plane but did not know which person it was. So we hit everybody."

The student said the defecting group seized control of the passenger cabin and threw open the door of the crews' compartment. There they found the man who turned out to be the security officer.

"The secret policeman was nearest the door," the student continued.

"He drew a small Browning pistol, but our leader smashed him over the head with his iron bar. We took the pistol and threatened the rest of the crew, making them move into the passenger compartment. Our leader fired a shot into the air, and everyone put up his hands.

"Our leader took the controls and brought the plane down low as we crossed the frontier five or ten minutes later."

The student said the plane circled Vienna and then crossed the Danube River, flying toward Germany.

"We did not know where we were," the Hungarian youth said. "We had no maps. But we saw the airfield here and hoped we were in West Germany."

The field the plane landed at is under construction as a North Atlantic Treaty Organization air base in southern Germany about ninety miles from the Czechoslovak frontier. Only the primary airstrip has been completed.

The West German police said there were two women aboard, a girl who was a member of the defecting group and an older woman.

At the Ingolstadt hospital, a doctor told reporters that none of the patients was in critical condition. Some of the injuries, including broken bones, were suffered when the occupants were hurled about the cabin while the plane was momentarily out of control, the doctor said.

According to the West German police, seven Hungarians requested asylum. The twelve others, including all crew members, asked to be returned to Hungary.

Other Flights Recounted

The seizure of the Hungarian airliner by anti-Communists recalled previous flights to freedom from behind the Iron Curtain.

In March, 1952, two Rumanian air officers captured a World War I bomber and flew it to Belgrade, Yugoslavia. A year later four Czechs took over a Czechoslovak airliner and landed it at Frankfurt, Germany. Twenty-three of the passengers on the plane decided to return to Czechoslovakia.

A third plane seizure took place in May, 1955, when two Rumanian flight instructors took a Navy training plane to the Turkish island of Kefken in the Black Sea.

Another spectacular escape occurred in September, 1951, when the engineer and thirty passengers took over a Czechoslovak train and brought it to West Germany. Eighty other passengers on the train returned to Czechoslovakia.

The accounts detailed in this book were covered by *Time Magazine* in their July 23, 1956 issue.

The article, titled "Hungary: Free-for-All to Freedom" can be found in their archive.

283

The New York Times

7 Seize Hungari In Midair Fight

San Antonio Expre

The Frederick po

BATTLE ON PLANE

Continued from First Page
fire, the ringleader knocked
him down.

from the Hungarian bord
and 50 miles from Munich.
Among those in the Ingo
stadt hospital was the secr

Wild Gun Fight in Clouds

Passengers Ta

INGOLSTADT, Germany, July ... The seven later were joined by t
draw to the passenger com-
partment, and took over the
controls.

The seven passengers wf
remained neutral asked to l
returned to Hungary.

...ured as Batt

ate Toughens

VOL. XLIX, NO. 177

2—IDAHO SUNDAY JOURNAL · Sunday, July 15, 1956

Seven Hungarians Grab Plan Make Flight to Free World

8 Seize Red Plane In Midair Battle, Fly It To Freedom

INGOLSTADT, Germany (AP)—
Seven desperate anti-Communists asked political asylum today after seizing control of a
Hungarian airliner in West Germany.
Twelve of the 19 m...
passenger... End of Bloody Flight to Freedom

student, said he had rela
in the United State. He al
a message to reporters as
them to contact Mrs. Willian
Farmer of Chicago.
said ...

Six passengers and officials after debarking from the seized Hungarian airliner near Ingoldstadt, Germany. The two on left side to return to Hungary while the others have asked asylum.

Escapees Say Bleak Future Led to Plane Plo

The Communist pilot of the seized Hungarian airliner and a passenger stand near plane shortly after it was landed in West Germany

INGOLSTADT, Germany, July 14
(AP)—Two of seven freedom-seek-
ing Hungarians said today "complete lack of hope for the future"
drove them to risk their lives by
capturing a Communist airliner in
mid-air.

The seven, who told German
police they hated communism,
crash-landed the American-built
DC3 of the Hungarian state airline
on an airfield near here last night.

They reached the West after a
bloody mid-air struggle in which
they subdued the crew of four and
eight other passengers, disarmed a
Communist secret police agent and
hedgehopped along the Danube

River out of Hungary, over Austria
and into West Germany.

All seven asked for political asylum. Bavarian state officials said
they had first to question the plot-
ters and the remaining 12 persons,
who have said they wished to return to Hungary, but expected the
asylum request would be granted.

2 More Ask Asylum

(Two passengers today decided to
join the ranks of the seven who
commandeered the plane and asked
for political asylum, UP reported.)

Five of the escapees are in the
hospital, together with seven other
passengers, suffering from injuries
received in the battle. Among

them is Gyorgy Polyak, a Wo
War II Hungarian Air Force pi
who led the plot and piloted t
plane to freedom after forcing t
Communist pilot from his seat
gunpoint.

There was one woman amo
the conspirators. She was Ens
Iszak, 19, wife of Ferenc Iszak,
25-year-old Budapest student w
was with her. Interviewed in t
hospital, where she was bei
treated for a broken finger a
broken ankle received in the fig
she said:

"The systematic destruction
Communist authorities of
(Cont. on Page 31, Col. 3)

EUROPEAN EDITION

THE STARS AND STRIPES

Unofficial Publication of the U.S. Armed Forces in Europe

Volume 15 Number 88 · 5 cents a copy · Sunday, July 15, 195

284

PHOTOS

The Aircraft

The official identification of the commercial aircraft was HA-LIG. For the purposes of this book the flight is identified as **"HA-LIG"** *operated by MALEV.*

The aircraft as it is parked on the tarmac of the Manching NATO Airbase (Ingolstadt, W. Germany).

Inside the disheveled passenger cabin.

The pried-open cockpit door.

The weapons:
From left: The Author's rusty weapon, Charlie's Club, The AVO Agent's gun.

The Author and his wife in a West German Hospital

Printed in the USA
CPSIA information can be obtained
at www.ICGtesting.com
JSHW022211140824
68134JS00018B/988

9 781630 478261